# Daughters & Dads

# Daughters & Dads

## BUILDING A LASTING RELATIONSHIP

## Chap & Dee Clark

NAVPRESS
BRINGING TRUTH TO LIFE
NavPress Publishing Group
P.O. Box 35001, Colorado Springs, Colorado 80935

## OUR GUARANTEE TO YOU

We believe so strongly in the message of our books that we are making this quality guarantee to you. If for any reason you are disappointed with the content of this book, return the title page to us with your name and address and we will refund to you the list price of the book. To help us serve you better, please briefly describe why you were disappointed. Mail your refund request to: NavPress, P.O. Box 35002, Colorado Springs, CO 80935.

The Navigators is an international Christian organization. Our mission is to reach, disciple, and equip people to know Christ and to make Him known through successive generations. We envision multitudes of diverse people in the United States and every other nation who have a passionate love for Christ, live a lifestyle of sharing Christ's love, and multiply spiritual laborers among those without Christ.

NavPress is the publishing ministry of The Navigators. NavPress publications help believers learn biblical truth and apply what they learn to their lives and ministries. Our mission is to stimulate spiritual formation among our readers.

www.navpress.com

Library of Congress Catalog Card Number: 97-44063

ISBN 1-57683-048-9

Photograph by Art Montes de Oca

Some of the anecdotal illustrations in this book are true to life and are included with the permission of the persons involved. All other illustrations are composites of real situations, and any resemblance to people living or dead is coincidental.

Clark, Chap, 1954–
    Daughters and dads : building a lasting relationship / Chap and Dee Clark.
      p.    cm.
    ISBN 1-57683-048-9
    1. Fathers and daughters—United States.   2. Parent and teenager—United States—Religious aspects—Christianity.
    I. Clark, Dee.   II. Title.
    HQ755.85.C57   1998
    306.874'2—dc21                               97-44063
                                                      CIP

Printed in the United States of America

2 3 4 5 6 7 8 9 10 11 12 13 14 15 / 05 04 03 02 01

FOR A FREE CATALOG OF
NAVPRESS BOOKS & BIBLE STUDIES,
CALL 1-800-366-7788 (USA)
OR 1-416-499-4615 (CANADA)

Published in association with the literary agency of
Wolgemuth & Hyatt, Inc., Brentwood, Tennessee

# Contents

# Foreword

Being good fathers to our sons is something that comes somewhat naturally to dads. We teach them to play football, how to change the oil, and model what it means to be men of God.

But in the midst of it all, we often lose sight of fathering our daughters. Feeling lost in the world of makeup, developing bodies, and bad hair days, we step back. We lose the emotional ties we had when they were little girls. They no longer climb up in our laps to share their secrets and we're unsure how to relate.

Fathers, this must change.

Our daughters desperately need us. They need our love, our attention, our hugs, and our friendship. In this truthful and poignant book, Chap and Dee Clark examine the relationship between father and daughter, shedding light on our fears and questions about our girls.

For fathers of young daughters, this book is a road map of what's ahead, showing detours around potential problems and disasters. For fathers of teenage daughters, this book is a wake up call to the important role we play in their lives. And for fathers of grown daughters, this book is a path toward healing as we make amends for past failures. My daughter, Kristy, is grown and has her own home and family. Yet, I have many opportunities to restore what was lost in previous years.

I pray that God will use this book to draw you and your daughter closer together and build a lasting relationship.

Bill McCartney

# Preface

Over the last two decades we have been involved in the lives of hundreds—perhaps many hundreds—of teenage girls. Through our work in local churches and with Young Life, a Christian organization that relationally seeks to introduce Jesus Christ to adolescents on their own turf, we've had the chance to hear and even experience firsthand how deeply daughters want to be close to their fathers. Several times we've wanted to help fathers see and understand just how powerful a force they are in their daughters' lives and what these young women want and need from the man they call Daddy. We trust that this book will be a helpful resource for the father who loves his daughter enough to provide her the leadership, friendship, and love she needs to prepare for healthy adulthood.

In a way, this book is born of five "parents": Our years spent in ministry with adolescent girls; our education and research (Dee holds an M.A. in counseling and is a therapist, and Chap has a Ph.D. in father-adolescent communication and is on the faculty of Fuller Seminary); Dee's history of growing up without the benefit of a father; and a daughter of our own who is just beginning the process of going through adolescence. The strongest fibers of the book, however, and where we got the idea in the first place, are the hundreds of letters we've received from adolescent girls across America during the last year and a half. After reading a few random letters that dealt with the relationships girls have (or would like to have) with their fathers, we began to see that many young people are more likely to write a letter to a stranger about their dads than they are to communicate directly with their fathers. This prompted us to begin soliciting letters wherever we went to speak, inviting girls to write a letter to their dads that they would not necessarily give to them. We received more than two hundred letters in a short time, and a few letters have been trickling in ever since. We have included many of these letters, changing only the names and specific cities while leaving the basic area of the country and the age of the writer.

Most of the letters were heartbreaking (we cried *a lot!*), and some were downright nasty. But many letters came from daughters who wanted to give their fathers the benefit of the doubt and yet honestly tell them something they needed to hear. The more letters we received, the more convinced we were of being on the right track. Indeed, fathers in America — even *churchgoing* fathers — need to hear what these young women have to say.

Nearly everything we assert in this book was either spawned or supported by one or more letters. The latest research on adolescent girls' developmental needs matched up completely with the letters we read (and many of these insights and results of years of study have yet to make it into even college textbooks on development).

Dee's experiences of growing up from the time she was five years old without much of a relationship with her father are reflected within each chapter in a sidebar called "From Dee: Memories of an Adult Daughter." These remembrances focus on Dee's reflections on how it felt not to have her father's support in relation to the issues presented in each chapter. Our intent is to sober fathers with a picture of just how serious and necessary their role is in their daughters' lives.

Society in general, and even some Christian leaders, may not believe that daughters need their dads, but social science—and, we believe, the Scriptures—clearly call fathers to love and stand with their kids, especially through the minefield of adolescence.

One last note: This book is overtly designed for fathers who are currently the parents of an adolescent girl. But everything stated herein is valuable for the father who has a younger daughter or whose daughter is no longer living at home. For the former, this book will help you get ready for the relational ride of your life! For the latter, it's never too late to reconnect with your daughter. Use the principles and letters in this book to reflect on how you are doing now as a father. Perhaps you could even use them as a springboard for a new round of talks. In short, every father of a daughter, this book is for you.

This book offers fathers an opportunity to hear from a few daughters out there who have stories to tell their own fathers but have a hard time, for one reason or another, being honest with them. For the dad who is reading this book, this is a chance to slow down and consider the gift God has given you in your daughter. She is a blessing, a joy, and a treasure. Be a steward of this treasure by asking God to help you get a firm grasp of the power of your role in her life. She will never let you forget it!

*Chap and Dee Clark*
*Englewood, Colorado*

# Acknowledgments

As we were finishing this book, we were presented with an offer to move from Denver to southern California. We have lived in Colorado for eleven years. We've raised our children here, built deep, lifelong friendships, and lived out of a rich and satisfying network of relationships. We love Denver, our friendships, and the life we have here; but somehow all five of us sensed that God was directing us to move. Because of this decision, we wish to dedicate this book to our Colorado friends and colleagues.

To our friends in and around the Downing House, Greenwood Community Church, and Young Life: Thank you for eleven years of friendship, fun, and adventure. We've loved the time we've spent with you and will cherish each opportunity we have to be together in the future.

To our couples group (known affectionately as "Bubbles"): When we first got together we never imagined we would go so deep or connect so intimately. Thank you all for the honesty, vulnerability, compassion, and commitment each of you has shown to us. To be known and loved by such a gifted and diverse group of people has helped us to grow up. We can't stop now, just because we're moving!

*Acknowledgments*

To the Denver Seminary community: Thank you for the six-plus years of serving together. We've learned a great deal and been encouraged to be ourselves and boldly use our gifts. We will miss you.

# CHAPTER ONE

# My Princess Is Growing Up

A few years ago, as I winged across the country on a commercial flight, I was blindsided by the reminder that my daughter and I are intimately and powerfully linked together.

Accompanying the airline's chicken salad croissant was a showing of the film, *Father of the Bride.* I'd seen it in a theater, and like most of the men I know who have daughters, I was moved as I watched that little girl become a woman in less than two hours. But on the airplane, one glance at the screen was all it took before I was hit with a roundhouse of emotion like none I'd ever felt. I had just kissed my daughter Katie goodbye, and I was perhaps only slightly aware of those mixed feelings I carried of longing and guilt for leaving her behind. There before my eyes was the cinematic evolution of child to adult, of princess to queen. The director took no prisoners. He knew his trade and milked the moment. As I watched the scene where the father (Steve Martin) remembers his daughter as a small child, then a preteen, an early adolescent, a high school beauty, and finally a woman, I saw my daughter. And I cried. No—I wept!

I was embarrassed and confused. I am not a man who cries

## From Dee
## Memories of an Adult Daughter

———

I remember my teen years like they were yesterday. Some days I felt like a little girl who wanted to stay home where I would feel safe and warm. Other days I resisted those walls and fought for independence and freedom. At times I just longed to be hugged; but sometimes I also felt awkward and resentful around everyone, feeling as if I was being treated like a child. Even now I can see myself pushing to make decisions for myself, claiming I was confident in my choices, but inside not being so sure. I carefully studied the words, dress, and lifestyle of my older sister and her friends, hoping to gain some tips on how to navigate my independence. It was so hard to grow up!

Horrified by one full year of being called "gorilla legs," I took the big plunge into womanhood by getting intimately acquainted with my new Lady Remington razor.

*(continued)*

a lot—those guys whom I verbally admire but often secretly disdain. Yet that day I had a hard time controlling myself. I'd been doing exactly what my culture told me to do—"provide for and protect" my family, the life task of the father—and yet I felt an emptiness and a deep sense of loss as I considered my little girl growing up. *She's leaving me,* I thought, *and I can't stop it!* My little "Angel Eyes," the special name we gave her when she was three years old, was growing up and leaving me behind.

I know that most fathers care, at least a little. But something happens to those men who love to be called "Daddy," whose hearts miss a beat with every hug, and whose eyes tear up when she says her prayers. A price must be paid for that kind of caring. As our daughters grow up, the wonder of innocence and the freshness of spirit are like a narcotic we want to harness, bottle, and keep handy for when we need a dose of goodness and a taste of heaven. Of course, mothers feel this way, too. But it's different for dads, because what we feel goes beyond pride to something it seems we're barely allowed to feel in our world—affection, tenderness, and intimacy. Our daughters represent a kind of intimate, innocent connection that gives us hope in an often lonely, hectic world.

What is your pet name for your daughter? The 1950s sitcom *Father Knows Best* made popular the name "Kitten", but

"Princess," "Angel," and "Pumpkin" all describe that same feeling a father has for his daughter: "You're something small, simple, and helpless. You are cute and warm and bring me great pleasure. You are my own treasure, to guard and protect, to cherish and hold, to watch over and defend."

This sense of fatherly protection/affection is fine when your daughter is three years old, or maybe even six. But soon she'll begin to want to break out of this "box" of love you've built and become more than a beautiful pet or a painting to be admired. She wants—and needs—to become a woman.

> *Dear Daddy,*
>
> *I know you love me, and that I can always count on your love. But I feel so small around you, like I'm your toy or something. I'm not a child—I'm fifteen—but to you I am your "little girlfriend." I'm not your little girlfriend! I want you to hold me and tell me you love me, but you have got to realize that you need to let me go!*
>
> *Please don't hate me for telling you this, but I would rather have you leave me alone than treat me like a child.*
>
> —Susan, age 15, Arkansas

Susan's letter reflects a conflict of powerful emotion for both a daughter and her

My body was starting to take on new shapes and perform functions that, quite honestly, grossed me out! I worried that my clothes weren't just right, my hair was too curly, and that a pimple might rear its ugly head right in the middle of my face. These were some of the darkest days of my life. I didn't necessarily want to talk about these things, I just needed to know someone was there for me.

Even the boys I grew up with suddenly seemed different. Without me even noticing, life began to change, and it seemed to happen out of nowhere. We all seemed different, traveling now in "packs"—girls with girls and boys with boys, sending conflicting messages back and forth. These were the same boys I had played soccer with for years. But now when they were around, my stomach got tight and I couldn't control my giggling. Everything around me was changing. I was terrified and ecstatic at the same time.

During those turbulent years, I felt strangely disconnected from Mom, and I wished Dad was around

*(continued)*

*(continued from previous page)*
more. I always wanted to have the kind of relationship with him in which we could talk about some of these feelings, but he seemed so nervous and distant around me. Even now I wonder if he might have helped me understand those strange new feelings. But that didn't happen. My dad wasn't there for me when I needed him.

———

father—an emotion neither one is prepared for. The move from child to woman is a confusing process at best, yet every family with a daughter goes through it. For most of these families it hurts a little, for some it hurts a lot. A few families pretend it makes no difference. But it always makes a difference for the daughter!

As his daughter grows up, these years make their mark on a father's heart in three ways: (1) the realization of lost innocence, (2) the stark reality that nothing stays the same, and (3) the confusion of conflicting emotions and relational roles as his precious little girl is becoming a woman.

### The Realization of Lost Innocence

Dee and I have spent our adult lives working with and caring for young people. Although I should be used to it, there remains for me an emotional struggle as I watch girls enter sixth grade as (usually) wide-eyed children with sweet, innocent faces, and leave eighth grade as savvy veterans of growing up in America.

By the time today's children have reached high school, no dark corner of humanity's shadows remains that they have not heard and learned about, if not seen and experienced firsthand. The innocence of childhood is being lost in today's uncensored society. Author and speaker Mike Yaconelli tells the story of two five-year-olds talking. One says to the other, "I found a condom on the patio," to which the other replied, "Neat! Uh, what's a patio?"

Consider for a moment what your daughter was like at age seven. Do you remember conversations with her about the complex world into which she was entering? Did a television show or commercial cause her to ask a question about sex, divorce, racism, hatred, or human cruelty? Perhaps she hardly ever asked, but you knew that she wanted you to help her understand how life can sometimes be so ugly, dark, and random. You are not alone if those conversations were rare or even nonexistent because most men in our culture are uncomfortable when it comes to these types of discussions. But can you remember having the *feeling* that you really wanted to say *something?* Can you recall a time when you first woke up to the fact that the little girl whose diapers you studiously avoided changing was suddenly and forcefully being "thrown to the wolves" of contemporary culture? Were you scared? Sad? Or, as with so many fathers, did you attempt to turn off the internal switch of despair, hoping your fear would just go away?

Jennifer is sixteen going on twelve. Her parents have always been afraid of what the culture might do to their daughter if it wrapped its ugly tentacles around her soul. From the time she was a little girl, Jennifer was told about the dark, hostile world that awaited her innocent and tender spirit. Her pastor was aware of this parental fear, and the youth minister at their church felt the pressure to help protect Jen from anything that might damage her God-given innocence. To date, Jennifer has not been allowed to watch television without her parents, to go on a date (or even to consider a romantic relationship), to attend youth group meetings without prior parental consent regarding content, or to have any friends whom her parents deem unacceptable (defined as those whose families do not conform to their family's standards). She was allowed to go to a conference this past summer, but her parents came with her, "to make sure she was not exposed to anything that might harm her."

Jennifer came up to me following a message I had delivered. She wasn't crying, but she displayed a chilling sense of despair. In explaining her family to me, she first wanted me to know that her parents loved her. Her dad, however, had such a fear of the "world" that she felt smothered, overly sheltered, and ill-prepared for life. She was speaking to me because I had referred to those who have received Christ as "bread to a starving world." She said that she didn't know many nonbelievers, and those she did know she had been taught to avoid. She went on to explain that she wanted to go to college in two years, but her parents were afraid for her. The more she talked, the more desperate she became. As she walked away, I felt sad — for her and for her family. Fear had surrounded them like a blanket. Life was not a "grand adventure" as I had proclaimed during my talk; it was a defensive struggle for survival against a powerfully hostile world.

Perhaps Jennifer's story sounds extreme to you. Maybe you identify more with Meagan. She talked to me at the same conference.

Meagan says that her parents so completely trust her that she hasn't had a curfew or any parental restrictions since junior high school. With the skin around her nose ring slightly infected and her sagging pants indicating what has come to be known as an "alternative" lifestyle, Meagan was still a warm, sweet fifteen-year-old who carried a sheen of toughness as a consequence of her life choices. Meagan had a gentle heart underneath the makeup and, not unlike Jennifer, her story also made me sad.

Meagan told me that she knew her father loved her but he "wasn't very good at expressing it — he's a guy, you know?" When she was in seventh grade, her first boyfriend wanted her to drink alcohol, smoke cigarettes, and have sex with him. She felt uncomfortable with the situation and a bit confused and out of control, but she liked him. She thought about talking to her dad and even tried a few times, but he was obviously nervous about such matters and told her that whatever was bothering her, he had confidence she would do the right thing. However, Meagan wanted and needed more.

She decided to take one day at a time and do the best she could. This began for her a journey that included experimentation with alcohol and some drugs ("nothing real bad"), unhealthy friendships and social alliances ("I guess my friends haven't been the best"), and several sexual encounters ("It's hard to go back once you've been there"). Meagan lost her innocence at thirteen. Now a junior in high school, and all grown up, Meagan lived with the emotional and relational calluses of growing up too fast and too soon.

Two girls, two parental responses to a daughter's adolescent journey: Jennifer, sheltered to the point of being socially inept; Meagan, left to fend for herself without boundaries or guidelines. Two girls who are gently bitter, each believing they were let down by parents who love them.

Earl Palmer, pastor at University Presbyterian Church in Seattle, recently stated in an address to youth workers and parents: "We cannot nor should we try to prepare the road for the child. It is our job to prepare the child for the road." This is the task of parenting in a world where innocence is quickly lost. We must help our daughters know and understand how deeply they are loved and give them the foundational security to slowly take off the glasses of innocence in order to see the world as it is. We must be there with them and for them, as they slowly learn the difference between the ideal of God's desire in creation and the stark reality of humanity's selfishness and consequent brokenness.

Our role as parents is neither to throw a protective cover over our children's eyes and minds, as with Jennifer's family, nor to leave them to figure life out on their own, as with Meagan's parents. Rather, our role as fathers — and mothers — is to maintain a family environment where love, mercy, and kindness are the rule without closing our eyes to the plight of the world. When we love our "little girls," our role is hard to acknowledge and even more difficult to balance. But as our daughters grow up, we must be there to help them deal with the complex and confusing transition from the warmth of parental protection to the exposure of grown-up life.

### Nothing Stays the Same

There is no better demonstration of the word *cute* than a young girl all dressed up. When my daughter started dance lessons, I would find myself choking back tears every time the biannual recitals rolled around. Not tears of sadness, really. The word *melancholy* better describes it. Those precious, tender, sweet five-year-old darlings in makeup and lace were a stark reminder of what happens in every family. Those events were a wake-up call for me to life's ultimate reality: nothing you cherish stays the same (except, of course, for the consistent love and character of Christ; and as I change, even my understanding of that changes!).

This principle of change presents one of the most difficult aspects of being a daddy: The little girl who fell asleep on my lap, the precious angel who loved to finger paint personalized Picasso-like originals, the innocent cherub who couldn't wait for the kiss *and* the present when I came in from out of town now has a miniskirt in the closet, a boyfriend with an earring, and a nearly psychotic fear of being seen with me in public! My baby is changing right before my eyes!

In 1991, pollster George Barna offhandedly remarked on a syndicated radio program, "The next decade will be the most important decade in the history of humanity." He went on to assert that the rapid changes in information distribution, financial complexity, and societal structure would cause a fundamental shift in how every person orders his or her life. "Change is inevitable," he claimed, "and we must be ready for the changes that come."

For fathers, this obvious truth meets emotional, if not intellectual, resistance. Everyone knows that life is about change and movement and growth. But when you love something, when you cherish what is happening right now, it's hard to accept and honor change. Like the video collage in *Father of the Bride,* we all want to grab hold and not let go of the process of our daughters growing from little girls into women. Although each stage of life has its own set of unique joys and lasting memories, in the midst of one of these stages—especially with girls—many fathers will want to wrap the memory, store it away in a safe place, and preserve it. We want to render it untouchable by time and life experience.

Inevitably, little girls become big girls, then young women, and, eventually, fully grown women. The father who understands this and has the resolve and emotional energy to accept life's changes and prepare for them will be able to build a deeper, more powerful set of memories of life with his daughter. And he will send her off into the world of adulthood a healthy, capable woman.

Change is inevitable. A daughter will become a woman. As she begins to think for herself, to assert herself, a father's role changes. He can be a friend, an ally, and a trusted confidant if he recognizes that change will come. The stakes are high. The woman God has given you needs to know that you believe in her, trust her, and care enough to help her to experience the fullness of God's dream for her.

### A Father's Confusion

The third area where a father feels his daughter's move from child to woman is in the sheer confusion this life transition creates for him. Every dad knows how to hold, cuddle, and play with his baby girl. As she gets older, this relationship obviously changes. No one would argue that some father-daughter activities and behaviors are appropriate with a child but not with a teenager. For instance, a six-year-old sleeping on her father's lap presents a beautiful picture of nurture and love. That picture with a sixteen-year-old would raise some eyebrows. There's no mystical cutoff date for any given activity, but over time a father and his daughter will relate to one another in a different way from before. Often this change goes unnoticed and unspoken. But it's there.

Several studies have demonstrated that today's fathers want

to be better at the role than their own fathers. Historically, social scientists ignored a father's role and influence. But starting in the late 1980s, family researchers began to take a deeper look. Even as early as 1986, psychologist Stanley Cath discovered that most men felt that their own fathers had let them down, and many were determined they wouldn't do the same with their children. His findings have been affirmed consistently in subsequent studies.[1]

It is also true that many men are frustrated with this "new role" or at least their perception of it. Research has also shown that while men may desire to be better fathers than their own fathers, their behavior has not caught up with this desire. Many men haven't yet figured out how to be the father they say they want to be. A man may desire to relate to and nurture his own children better than his own father nurtured him, but he's also likely to be unaware of how he will accomplish his goal. If he's not aware of how his children—especially daughters—perceive him, as well as what they are going through and need from him, he will be unable to fulfill his desires as a father.

Several deeply buried but everpresent questions haunt the modern father: "What does it mean to be the dad of an adolescent girl?" and "What does a father need to be and do differently as his daughter grows up?"

While popular theories abound regarding the role of fathers, few men understand where they can go to become more equipped. Most fathers want to be supportive, involved, and have a nurturing influence on their children. But exactly what daughters need is often a mystery to them. It's one thing to raise a son—after all, nearly every father was at one time a son himself! But raise a daughter? This is a different ballgame altogether. Dr. Bruce Narramore pointedly synthesizes the issues facing today's fathers:

> Our society requires seventeen years of education before certifying a person to teach in public school. Medical

doctors and psychologists must have twenty years of schooling before they practice on your children. And many states require teenagers to take a course in driver's education before they can be licensed to drive a car. But to rear children from the cradle to their twenties, our society doesn't require one hour of formal training.[2]

Some men, then, simply plow ahead, presuming there is really no difference between raising a son and raising a daughter. However . . .

Kristy's dad wanted to be close to her. He had raised two sons and he felt he'd done a pretty good job. He was still close with both boys. They had basically stayed out of trouble and they were doing well in college. Now that they were gone, his attention turned to Kristy. But for her, it was too little too late.

Kristy's letter reflects pain and disappointment as she seeks to help her father understand what she wants and needs from him:

Dear Dad,

I'm tired of trying to compete with my brothers for you. Now that they are gone, you want me to be just like them. But I'm not just like them! A long time ago I wanted you to talk to me, and to listen to me. But you were too busy with Jeff and Tim—going to games, coaching their sports, and playing golf. Now that they're gone, it's my turn. But I don't really want to do things, I just want you to know me. I love you, Dad, and I know you are trying (sometimes too hard!). But you need to stop, Daddy, stop and listen to me.

—Stacy, 14, Orlando, FL

Stacy's letter is a cry to be noticed, to be taken seriously. Her father may be confused over his role, but she's ready to forgive him and move on. Her love for him is stronger than her disappointment and frustration.

Without exception, the letters we've received from daughters have expressed a desire for reconciliation and a fresh start with their dads. Every daughter we've heard from wanted to connect with her father, regardless of circumstances or history.

Face it. If you are a dad, change is inevitable. Your daughter's innocence will eventually give way to knowledge, and you may not know exactly what to do as her father. But don't let that stop you! Your little princess is growing up and she needs her daddy!

# CHAPTER TWO

# "I Need You, Daddy!"

*Dear Daddy,*
*I guess you don't need me to tell you, but I'm growing up.*
*I used to love to sit on your lap and listen to you tell me*
*stories, but now I just don't. I want you to realize that I*
*am a young woman, and that I know what I am doing.*
*When I cry, I don't need you or Mom to "fix it." I may*
*just want to cry! You were such a good dad when I was*
*little—you used to be fun and funny and I liked to listen*
*to you tell your dumb stories. But now I'm getting older*
*and don't really need anybody to tell me stories. I just*
*want you to know this stuff.*

—Phylis, 12, Nashville, TN

Not long ago, the people of Boulder, Colorado, were rocked by the news that a young girl was brutally raped and murdered in her own home. The striking thing about her was the extraordinary life this little girl had lived. She was a rising star in the world of child beauty pageants. Photographs of her enraptured and enraged a nation—a six-year-old dressed up in a sequined gown, a hairstyle more fitting for the senior prom than the playground, and enough properly applied makeup to physically attract the most hardened or even virtuous of men. In short, the videos and pictures of this angel-seductress only added to the intrigue of this cruel and tragic event.

We watched the news, waiting for an arrest and ultimate conviction, but the lingering memory of the beauty-child remains fixed. She had grown up way too fast. The dads of girls I know all felt the same as they watched the spectacle: *It won't be long until my little girl is wearing makeup and walks out the door dressed like a grown woman going out on the town.*

For dads, little girls are the epitome of innocence and beauty. Every father knows the feeling of having his little princess run across a room to jump into his arms and kiss him on the cheek. There are very few sounds that can rival a daughter's delighted squeal—"Daddddddyyyyyyy!"—when he comes home from a long day of fighting the battles of the world. The warmth of her embrace, the touch of her cheek against his—these are what every father loves and holds dear in his heart.

When she is young, a daughter is something soft and gentle, small and frail, innocent and precious. She's like a figurine on the mantel to be aggressively guarded, as well as tenderly cherished.

The intuitive father also knows that

this gentle beauty he holds is far more excited about the idea of closeness with him than she is about the reality. When she falls off her bike or kids make fun of her in school, she runs to her mom. Dad may personify for her the idea of safety and warmth, but the stronger bond still remains with Mom. Sure, she loves her dad, often with passion and abandon. But her heart still belongs to her mother.

and to encourage me.

I know now that God created in me a longing to be close to my dad, but I didn't know it then. He was too disconnected and too involved in his own world to be my rock or comfort. I often wondered, *Who can I trust to help me find my way through these changes?* I felt so alone.

During the childhood years, this mother-daughter bond is unique. It is a secret world where a man, even Dad, is not invited. Every father senses it, and most fathers appreciate it, but the relationship is undeniably closed. From shopping, dressing up, and "doing her hair," to endless conversations about boys and friends and fears and rivals, mothers have an "in" that serves to keep fathers away. But something begins to happen around age ten or eleven to this mother/child bond. In some cases this may manifest itself in a daughter seeing her mother shift from friend to rival, confidant to opponent.

When daughters begin the adolescent journey, everything starts to change. And it's the rare family that is prepared for the coming relational storm.

Dee and I are involved as volunteers in a junior high outreach ministry called, appropriately enough, Wild Life. For the past four years we've watched a remarkable and seemingly overnight change occur as sixth-grade girls enter our lives only to leave as sophisticated, budding young women. As we watch this metamorphosis, one thing invariably stands out: The adult exterior is but a thin veneer covering a fragile person who still feels and even often acts like a little girl. The physical changes her body experiences are deceiving to her and the world around her, for her mind, heart, and spirit have yet to catch up with the new woman who is emerging.

Along with the physical changes, she is also beginning to feel a developmental difference inside. She begins to realize that she's no longer a little girl, yet she doesn't understand what the new world of womanhood will be like. The newness of this process, and the convoluted mixture of fear and excitement it brings, causes emerging young women to question just about everything. Like the newborn butterfly that pushes out of the warmth and safety of a cocoon, your daughter often feels as if she's seeing and experiencing life for the first time. Believe it or not, Dad, she longs to grab you by the hand as she takes her first steps as a woman.

> Dear Daddy,
> You have always been my hiding place. I remember when I was a little girl, scared or lonely, and I would crawl up into your lap, just to be reassured that you were there. But now it's different. You still want me to crawl in your lap. But I don't want to sit in your lap. I'm growing up, and you can't even see it! Why can't you just talk to me, listen to me, or just treat me like a person instead of your stupid "little princess"? Come on, Dad. Get a clue!
>
> —Julie, 15, Chicago, IL

Julie's letter presents a common dilemma that adolescent girls feel during this time of transition. Julie *loved* the times she shared with her dad, the cuddling and being close, the tickling and the quiet talks. But something is changing, and she's scared. More important, her frustration shows that she understands it little more than her father does. She's mad at him because he treats her with tenderness and affection! He's probably reeling as he wonders, *What have I done? Why is she running from me? Why doesn't she know that I love her and want to do the best I can to comfort her?*

This response helps neither Julie nor her dad. She wants more from him, not less! She needs him to treat her differently now that she has embarked on this new emotional adventure called adolescence. As a little girl, she needed her dad only for physical comfort and assurance. Now she wants him to take her seriously, to show her he cares about what she thinks as well as how she feels, to allow her to grow beyond the little girl he has always protected, just by being her dad.

As your daughter enters adolescence, she starts to drop little hints everywhere she goes. Telltale signs include outbursts of unexplained anger or depression, radical mood swings, and sometimes a noticeable chip on her shoulder. It seems as if she's just daring you to take her on. But just as quickly as you identify a sign of her emerging womanhood, she just as quickly reverts to being a cuddly little "princess" again, wanting to be held and hugged and led. Parents who are unaware of the reason for these frequent changes are often frustrated with such a seemingly schizophrenic child. Sometimes parents overreact to the point of actually hindering the growth process. The parents who know that a daughter's behavior is simply a marker of a major life transition will be able to help her make the most of this exciting yet frightening time.

### The Story of Scott and Jill

Scott's daughter Jill was twelve years old going on twenty when it hit them. Jill came downstairs on a Saturday afternoon visibly frustrated. Scott, who was watching a football game, noticed she was bothered but he didn't think twice about it. More out of courtesy than compassion, he casually commented, "Can I do anything for you, honey?" Jill, who perhaps should have known that her dad didn't actually mean for her to sit down and talk about her confused array of feelings (at age twelve she was only learning), came into the room and started to tell him everything she was feeling. Scott was caught completely off guard. He'd looked forward to this game for weeks and didn't really want to be interrupted. After all, everything she was saying seemed to be fairly petty and relatively unimportant. So he pretended to listen and continued to watch the game.

Jill, being a young woman, took about thirty seconds to realize that her dad's concern rang hollow. He had no intention of listening to her story. Scott hadn't lied. He had just implied a willingness to be there for her although he really wasn't all that interested. When she slowed her monologue and hesitated in the recounting of her day, Scott did what many men are so good at. Without looking up from the game, he offered her a terse, fifteen-second, quick-fix piece of advice: "Just call her and tell her you'll go with someone else to the party!"

At first Jill just sat there, stunned. Then she meekly walked out of the room, mumbling, "You never listen to me . . . you don't even care . . . all you care about is your stupid game."

Scott barely heard her and felt quite good that he had been a compassionate and available dad. And he hadn't missed much of the game to boot!

Of course you can see what's coming. But when you're in the thick of life, not actively prepared to be a father to your daughter, would you have responded any differently?

A father must provide his daughter three important elements as she begins this journey. First, he must take her seriously. Second, he must care about what she thinks. Third, he must be committed to walking with her through the journey of adolescence.

### Taking Your Daughter Seriously

When a child enters adolescence, the key word for her is *independence*. This is the essence of the adolescent quest—to be treated as and to feel like an individual who matters (often, of course, while blending into the crowd and not being noticed!). Fathers are among the greatest offenders at the outset of this process. Although you may mean well, Dad, it's truly amazing what you will say when you don't recognize just how fragile and needy your daughter is.

Like Scott, we fathers tend to forget that our daughters honestly need us to care about them. That means caring about the things they care about. Our daughters need to know that they are not just interruptions, they are one of the highest priorities in our lives. This is especially true for daughters in those most formative early teen years.

At this point your daughter doesn't really know what she needs or even wants. She's caught between two worlds. She feels a sense of comfort in the world of childhood; it's the world she knows and understands. But the new world of imminent adulthood is frightening and overwhelming, even as she intuitively knows it is right and exciting to enter it. Because of this tension, your daughter may subconsciously revert to the safety and protection of childhood, even as she is compelled to press on. This will cause her to constantly contradict herself. She'll be happy at five o'clock and depressed at six. She'll kiss you then turn around and yell at you. As she pushes you away and then tugs at your heartstrings, remember one thing: She loves you and needs you to take her seriously!

Daddy,
When I was little you called me "Daddy's little girl." We walked hand-in-hand through the mall, your big hand holding mine. All my dreams and fears were expressed to you. When I was with you I felt as if nothing could harm me. When I started to get older I pushed you away. You usually would have put your arm around me, but you soon stopped trying. I couldn't express my feelings to you anymore and my emotions seemed to be crazier than ever. Daddy, I still wanted you to hold me and call me Daddy's little girl. But I was so confused inside. I wanted to hold your hand and tell you everything. I saw your face when I

*went through that time in my life and I just wanted to apologize. Daddy, I know you just don't know what to say so I'll say it. I love you and I need to be your little girl.*

—Brittany, 17, Oklahoma City, OK

### Caring About What She Thinks

The second way you can begin to be the kind of father your daughter needs is to let her know that her opinions and ideas are important to you. For some fathers—perhaps most fathers—this can be a difficult task, especially in early adolescence, as she continually vacillates between being the logical, rational, and clear-thinking girl you knew so well just a few short years ago, and the incoherent, emotional, distracted "Dr. Jekyll and Mr. Hyde" with whom you now live! Most dads have very little patience with this and mistakenly mention it to their wives and even their daughters.

A friend recently clued me in on a television cartoon show that is popular with younger kids (and many of their parents): "Animaniacs." One of the minor characters is Katie Ka-Boom, a teenager who has an amazing character trait. When her parents don't seem to understand her, or they frustrate her, she turns into a monster and explodes. When the dust clears, she's standing in the midst of the rubble with her mom, dad, and little brother cautiously looking on. Then she says, "Nothing's wrong!"

The explosion of adolescence can cause a family to feel like they've been blown apart. Does this scenario sound familiar? Your thirteen-year-old daughter gets off the phone after talking with a friend and now has to decide whether or not she "likes" a boy who "likes" her. (In our community it's called "going out," and these relationships often last as long as two weeks!) She comes downstairs and tells you about the conversation. She speaks calmly and clearly, and she's able to sift out what is important and what she values. She seems to be on a track of making a wise, albeit juvenile, decision regarding this snot-nosed kid who has never said "boo" to her. You hear her out and tell her it sounds like she's doing a good job of thinking through the issues. As she happily goes upstairs to bed, you think to yourself, *Ah, my little girl is growing up. She's learning how to make good decisions.* When you kiss her goodnight and say a prayer with her, you go to bed confident that she's becoming all you ever dreamed her to be.

The next night she is quiet at dinner. You, being the nurturing father of the new millennium, ask how it's going with her new love interest. She stares down at her untouched food, her chin begins to quiver, and she suddenly erupts with what is to you an hysterical, irrational outburst of anger toward you (although later she says that she simply "got a little emotional"). She storms up the stairs, reminding the family in no uncertain terms (and in particular you, Dad) that nobody understands her and it's just fine if she'll never be able to get a boyfriend, and she probably won't ever get married (and you, Dad, are the reason) and she'll probably end up as a nun! (Door slams.)

Stunned, the family looks at you, wondering, some aloud, "What did you say to her?" Or worse, "What did you do to her!" You sit there, completely baffled. You've changed from Ann Landers to Attila the Hun in less than twenty-four hours.

Now is the moment that marks the kind of father your daughter wants and so desperately needs. Now is not the time to take her words personally or to get angry or to tell her, "Grow up!" Obviously, something has happened to hurt her, and she needs a place where she can express her pain, fear, and insecurity. For some completely irrational reason, she's chosen you as the focal point for all of her anxiety and frustration (and if you make yourself a willing mark by caring, you can be sure that when she needs a target, you may get hit).

Right now, what she needs is to know that you care about what she thinks, even if it's contradictory, confusing, or illogical.

Her desire is that you will take the time to listen and try to understand what she's thinking and feeling. She doesn't want answers, advice, or platitudes. She wants you to care about what she thinks.

The caring dad in this scenario would wait a few minutes and then go to her room. He would gently knock and ask permission to enter her private world. Even though she may not seem to want to talk, in most cases she will. (When she doesn't, it may have more to do with the timing than the desire to open up and connect.) Now is the time to simply say something like, "Honey, I sure haven't intended to upset you. If my question hurt you, I'm sorry." This could be followed up by, "Do you want to talk?" The important thing is that she knows she matters to you and that you're not trying to pry your way into her life. She just needs to know that you care and that you're willing to enter her world of hopes and fears, dreams and disappointments. This is the most precious gift you could ever give your daughter as she grows up.

### Walking with Her Through the Journey of Adolescence

As your daughter enters adolescence, a subtle shift takes place: She inherently needs and usually desires a unique relationship with her father.

Although her mother remains a significant figure in her life, it is at this stage that she longs for her daddy to treat her differently, to relate to her in a more grown-up way, and to trust and encourage her as she navigates the minefield of adolescence. Her need for him to treat her as a young woman instead of his "little princess" (though she hopes his adoration for her will never wane) is at the core of this budding stage of development. She needs to feel like she's more than a cute little doll. She wants her father to see her as an emerging young woman who has gifts and talents and the strength to make her mark on the world.

Although there's some truth in the idea that this is a private journey, no life quest is truly a private affair. We walk where others have walked. There are other travelers alongside us, before and behind us. A daughter's journey through the twisting, exhilarating, and sometimes painful wilderness of adolescence can be a living abyss when she feels she's undertaking it alone. Yet the sad fact is that many young women feel alone much of the time. For most there is always Mom. But an integral part of an adolescent girl's process is to identify herself as distinct from her mother. Even friends find it hard to travel this journey together, for each individual is required to follow her own path toward womanhood.

Who can provide her comfort and hope in the journey? We believe that God has designed the father to take on that crucial role as his daughter moves through adolescence. She needs a teacher more than a judge, a guide more than a boss, and a friend more than a protector. For this to happen, she needs a dad who is willing to walk beside her during these years. Unfortunately, as Terry Apter points out, for most girls this is rare:

> Fathers are often less involved with their daughters during their teenage years than they have been up to that point. Studies show that while fathers tend to be extremely attached and involved with their [young] daughters, closeness diminishes as girls reach puberty and adolescence. Girls talk to their fathers less, tell them less about their lives, spend less time with them, and in return receive less support and encouragement from them.[1]

You can be a different kind of father. If you choose to do so, you can look beyond the incongruity of her behavior and see past her tendency to push you out of her life. Remind yourself how difficult this time is for her, and remember that she loves you and needs you. Many times she doesn't want to tell you or she won't be able to find the words to express her need for you. But she desperately wants you to care, and she longs for your approval and your friendship.

> Daddy:
> I don't know where to start . . . there is so much I want to tell you about the real me, but you only see me as your "little girl." In fact, we've even joked about it before.
> I remember when we first moved to Kansas. I was growing out of the back rub stage, but I guess the move made me need you even more. You wrote me a letter when I was eight, commenting on this, but I still needed those back rubs. You sent me the letter nine years later and I read it for the first time a week ago. I sobbed when I read it. I realized that every once in a while I still need a daddy to take me in his arms and protect me from this awful world and keep me out of harm's way. Yet I need a father, too. Someone who will prepare me for the real world. Daddy, will you be my father, too?
>
> —Sally, 17, Lawrence, KS

# CHAPTER THREE

# Trust: The Glue That Holds Relationships Together

*Dear Daddy,*
*When I was little, you always told me that the most*
*important thing for me was to tell you the truth and*
*that you wanted to know you could trust me. Because you*
*lied to me about [my brother], I don't know if I can trust*
*you! Because of what you have done, I'm not sure I can*
*trust you with anything anymore. And you need to know*
*that it hurts really bad!*

—Marie, 16, Colorado Springs, CO

Trust is a precious but fragile gift. It takes years to earn, yet it can be destroyed in seconds. When Marie handed me that letter, it was obvious that she had been weeping. She *wanted* to trust her father with sensitive information, but somehow his response had produced a serious violation of one of Marie's most deeply cherished values, a value that her father had worked so hard to instill in the first place!

Webster's dictionary defines *trust* as "confident expectation." For a daughter to allow herself to draw close to her father and

## From Dee
### Memories of an Adult Daughter

Sometimes when I was a teen, it was just easier not to have any expectations of Dad. Then I wasn't disappointed when he let me down. (Even as I write these words, I know deep in my heart that what I'm saying is a lie; he *did* let me down, and it *did* hurt.) My relationship with Dad was distant and impersonal. I rarely saw him, and when I did he didn't seem to take me very seriously. Instead, I remember feeling like a child around him.

Many times I *wanted* to talk to him and get to know him. But as I look back I could sense that, as much as he told me he loved me, he never seemed willing to open up to me to talk about anything real or personal. I guess it was easier and safer for both of us to keep conversations on the surface. By not talking about real issues and feelings, he was never stuck with not knowing how

*(continued)*

open herself up to his influence in her life, she must have an unshakable confidence that he will take her seriously, treat her tenderly, and be unconditionally committed to her throughout these years. She must be convinced that when she lets him into the morass of thoughts and feelings that adolescence brings, he will be very careful. Most fathers would be shocked to realize how little their daughters trust them. Marie was not alone.

Dear Dad,
I'll never understand where I stood in your life. Every time I tried to talk to you, you wouldn't look up from your paper, or you turned away. I do remember a few meals together— sitting at the dinner table with a broken shoulder and being told to "sit still" because it was "my own stupid fault!" I do remember getting mostly straight A's in school but you only asking, "Why did you get a B in (fill in the blank)?" I never felt that you knew anything about me. I wanted to tell you about me, get your advice, but I just didn't know what you would say or think about me. . . .

—Elisabeth, 19, Atlanta, GA

From this letter it's impossible to tell what kind of father this man is. Were these normative events that simply serve as examples of a broad-stroke pattern, or were they isolated incidents that happen to have been crystallized in Elisabeth's memory? If the former is the case, the issue in their relationship is not so much a matter of trust as it is a general disregard and lack of care for his daughter. But perhaps this dad is actually a good, conscientious father. Maybe he cared about her but had a few bad moments. Every father slips up once in a while and fails in his relationship with his daughter, and he will occasionally hurt her. But when she is hurt and trust is broken, he must take proactive steps to repair the relationship.

The issue of trust is not always related to a specific incident or event. It may represent a growing internal sense of betrayal based on years of a daughter's careful observation of her father.

> *Dear Dad,*
> *Sometimes I feel that you love me but you don't respect what I say because I'm a girl. At least that's what I get from how you always listen to and respect my brother but not me.*
>
> —Kristen, 15, New Jersey

to answer my questions. He didn't have to be accountable for any of his own mistakes . . . like leaving me, my mom, and my sister.

Sitting in my room at his house after another weekend of superficial conversation and meaningless activity, I wondered if things were ever going to change between us. I wanted a relationship with him, but I couldn't tell if he wanted one with me. Did he even realize I was growing up? Did he ever sense my desire to know him and to be known by him? Could I ever be honest with him about my life and my anger at him for what he had done? I now know it would have been so easy to forgive him and to be close to him if only he had *tried* to get to know me. I wanted so badly to tell him of my plans, to hear his advice, to receive his approval.

Instead, I was left with a void—a hole in my heart that still causes pain.

———

Girls who grow up with a brother near the same age frequently struggle with what they see their brother getting from Dad and what they *perceive* they are not getting from Dad by comparison.

When we conducted a comprehensive research study on the differences between the way adolescent brothers and sisters perceive their individual relationships to their fathers, we found that more than 99 percent of the time boys reported a closer relationship to their dads than did their sisters. This was true regardless of what their respective ages were and who was older (as long as they were between twelve and nineteen and still living at home with their biological fathers). In terms of trust, daughters overwhelmingly reported they had less trust of their father than did the brothers (98 percent).

Our research team had some hints that there might be small differences between how boys and girls view their relationship to their fathers, but no one had yet studied brothers and sisters in the same family with the same father. The huge difference in reported closeness (or attachment) took the research team off guard. However, one message was loud and clear: Fathers somehow relate differently to sons than to daughters during the adolescent years. Their daughters sense this and it seems to cause them to back off from trusting their dads.

One more letter presents another issue that affects trust. This from an unnamed twelve-year-old girl whose parents were fighting to the point of separation.

*Dear Daddy,*

*Both of you get angry with me for doing stuff you don't like with my "bad" friends. Maybe they are bad; probably they are. But what reason have you given me to think you care? And they have problems, too; why shouldn't I hang out with kids like me? They accept me as I am. They don't criticize.*

*The thing is, kids should love their fathers. And I don't know if I love you. Maybe if you died I would cry, and realize how much I did love you. But right now, when my mind is clouded only by sadness and grief, I find I don't. I don't even like you very much. I can barely tolerate you in the same room with me.*

—No name given, 12, Dallas, TX

Although the letters are written from different angles, all of them point to an eroded trust in fathers.

Trust is a funny concept. We all so desperately desire that those closest to us trust us, yet our trust in them is often fragile and easily shattered.

Most dads would probably not even consider that their daughters might not trust them. At least that's the case with the fathers we've spoken to. Perhaps you're thinking that you've loved your little girl since she was born. You cuddled her, changed her diapers, took her on walks, played with her on your knee. As she grew, you told her she was beautiful, watched her dance or play soccer, and helped her with her math homework. But once she hit adolescence, it may have become harder to show your love for her.

Maybe she doesn't want to sit on your lap anymore or tell you about her life. Could it be that your little girl has needed something from you that goes deeper than "watching" her during activities and helping her out with the mundane tasks of life? For her to experience the best life has to offer her, she needs to know that she can trust her father.

## A Two-Way Street

Every relationship begins with trust. Your daughter needs and powerfully desires to trust you. But here is the real dichotomy: Your daughter not only wants to trust you, she also desires *you* to trust *her*! The issue of trust is a two-way street, but it is the rare parent and child who recognize this.

Whether or not you know it, your daughter wants your stamp of approval, your unconditional acknowledgment that you believe in her. As Doug Webster points out in *Dear Dad:*

*What Kids Want Their Fathers to Know,* kids (both boys and girls) want two things from their fathers: "Trust me" and "Leave me alone." As Webster presents what adolescents want to say to their fathers, he goes on to say that kids want "a dad who trusts his kids to grow up on their own."[1]

In this definition, trust is equated with giving a child the room to make decisions on her own. But I think this definition misses the core of trust, which is less about control and more about relationship. Your daughter wants to know that you trust *in* her far more than you intrinsically trust her *behavior.*

All children are looking for parents who will care more about character and heart than choices and lifestyle. Social scientists affirm that behavior and lifestyle are symptomatic of something going on inside. In other words, there is a reason for everything we do. But when your daughter says that she wants you to trust her, she's saying that she needs to know you believe in and trust *her,* even when you can't (or shouldn't) trust her *behavior* (and might even have to discipline her).

Now, as much as she wants you to trust her, your daughter is also longing to trust you. This idea of mutual trust is so important for kids that much of their self-esteem and healthy sense of personal power is directly associated with the perception of the trust they have in their dads.

This is how it works: If a twelve-year-old girl trusts her father to tell the truth, to be honest, to show respect, and to be gentle even in the midst of failure and mistakes, and if her dad seeks to understand what she is going through, it is far more likely that she will let him into her life. If this father proactively works to assure the reinforcement of this perception as she moves through adolescence, her confidence in him as a leader and guide will allow her the emotional freedom to open up to him, even when life gets messy and painful.

If, on the other hand, a girl approaches the teen years with a perception of her father as a distant, controlling, and argumentative dictator, she will not trust him with her emotions, decisions, and failures. As she grows up, she will look for someone to replace the male assurance she wants from her dad. Although she deeply wants Dad's guidance, counsel, and approval, if she doesn't trust him to care for her with gentleness and respect, she will look elsewhere.

Today's daughter needs a father who takes the time to stop, listen, and respond with great mercy and warmth. That's what trust is. The father who has built into his daughter the ability to trust *him* will not need to question whether or not he can trust *her!*

## The Three Dimensions of Trust

Adolescent behavior is, by nature, haphazard and erratic. That's why it's called *adolescent* behavior (as opposed to *adult* behavior)! During these years of transition, your daughter will make poor choices; she will fail and disappoint both you and herself. You must regularly address the behavioral trust that gets eroded during down times or strengthened during victorious times, especially as it relates to privilege and responsibility. But the greater understanding of trust must be built on the deeper foundation of *relational* and *character* trust. *Respect, acceptance,* and *understanding* are three essential elements of such a trust relationship.

### Respect
After a presentation, one father approached me with scowling face and said, "My father taught me that respect is something to be earned, not granted!" This dad was obviously taking issue with my encouragement to respect his daughter simply because she needed and deserved it.

As we talked, he became even more irate. In essence, he was having a hard time getting his fifteen-year-old daughter to perform on a level that warranted his idea of "earned respect." I asked him if we could see what the Scriptures taught, and he (reluctantly) agreed. We looked at these two passages:

> Show proper respect to everyone: Love the brotherhood of believers, fear God, honor the king. (1 Peter 2:17)
> Give everyone what you owe him: If you owe taxes, pay taxes; if revenue, then revenue; if respect, then respect; if honor, then honor. (Romans 13:7)

As we talked, he admitted that he wanted to freely offer his daughter the gift of respect, but he carried what he described as "an inner block" to such an idea. The longer we talked, the more he softened, and it became clear that he loved his daughter so much that the way he showed his love to her was how he had received love from his own father: You must perform, be good, live "holy," and then you will be worthy of my respect.

Once this father realized he was passing on his own father's philosophy of parenting, a style that had been so deeply destructive to himself, he was able to see how he had been treating his daughter and denying her what she truly needed. Once he realized this, he was able to take his eyes off himself and his own ingrained need to perform. Then he was able to rethink how he could show his daughter the respect she deserved. This father came to realize that love is hollow if respect is an elusive goal that must be earned by performance.

### Acceptance

*Dear Daddy,*
*I know that I have been a disappointment to you, especially lately. When you cried and told me that you could no longer trust me, and that you couldn't believe what I had done, I was so sorry. But when you went from*

*there and got mad, yelling, "How could you do this to me?" I kind of shut you out. I am sorry for what I did, and I will try not to do it again. But I'm also afraid now to tell you what's going on in my life because I'm not sure how you will take it. You always told me you want me to be honest, but can I really be honest with you? Can you handle it without taking it so personally?*

—Christine, 16, Madisonville, KY

Most people think that to accept means to condone. This is a battle the church has fought for centuries, and we will not solve it here. But there are two unmistakable factors that come into play with the whole idea of "acceptance."

The first is that our Lord modeled an acceptance of those who were considered "outside" of the religious and ethical boundary lines of the day:

The Son of Man came eating and drinking, and they say, "Here is a glutton and a drunkard, a friend of tax collectors and 'sinners.'" (Matthew 11:19)

He is also said to have "welcomed" such people—the "sinners" and "tax collectors"—who lived in apparent disrespect for morality and the law:

While Jesus was having dinner at Levi's house, many tax collectors and "sinners" were eating with him and his disciples, for there were many who followed him. When the teachers of the law who were Pharisees saw him eating with the "sinners" and tax collectors, they asked his disciples: "Why does he eat with tax collectors and 'sinners'?" On hearing this, Jesus said to them, "It is not the healthy who need a doctor, but the sick. I have not come to call the righteous, but sinners." (Mark 2:15-17)

In Luke 15, Jesus reveals to us the heart of God for those who have wandered away—those who are "lost" and those whose behavior has hurt others and been squandered on sinful living. If Jesus' understanding of those who fail and who are "lost" is that God loves and pursues them anyway, certainly our call as fathers is to pursue and welcome our daughters, even in light of disappointment, failure, and heartache.

The second factor that comes into play in understanding acceptance is our own deep need for the unconditional acceptance of our Father in heaven when we have failed Him. Each of us needs regularly to return to the cross and resurrection of Jesus to heal us of our own sin and lostness. If we were as sensitive to welcome and "eat" with our daughters, especially in their times of need and struggle, as God is with us when we fail or are broken, we would begin to get at the character of acceptance.

"Hate the sin, love the sinner." What a wonderful, neat, clean religious platitude. But what a difficult calling! If you want to build your daughter's sense of trust in you, then do whatever you can to communicate that you will *always* welcome her with open arms as her devoted father—even in the midst of failure or painful circumstances. This does not imply that her behavior will have no consequences. There may be times when you're forced to allow her to go her own way. But like the Prodigal's father, who kept his eyes on the road, waiting for his child's return (Luke 15:20-32), you must convince your daughter that you will always, unequivocally, accept her as your own when she needs to rest in your embrace.

### Understanding

Trust is withheld when there is fear of being misunderstood. Who hasn't had the experience of being misunderstood or misjudged? We've all been hurt by others who haven't taken the time to understand us or show gentleness and mercy when we're down. In order to trust someone, we must believe they know us well and what they don't know will make an effort to find out.

As with respect and acceptance, your daughter needs to know that you have some sense of who she is and what she feels. To trust you, she must have confidence that even if you don't understand something she does or says, you are willing to listen to her and to find out *her* perspective before you jump to give advice or draw conclusions.

*Dad,*

*Why do you insist on telling me what i'm thinking all the time? When you say that, it makes me want to run away from you. You think you know me and understand me, but you don't! Why don't you ask me questions before going off on one of your little speeches?*

*You don't like most of my friends, but at least they understand me. They listen, and they don't judge me. They just love me. You say you love me every day, but if you really did you would try to understand me.*

—Jennifer, 15, Denver, CO

There's no way around it. Understanding your daughter takes work. First, it means respecting her to the point of listening really hard! Second, it means that you have to gather all the facts, both objective and emotional, before you attempt interaction. And it means honestly trying to "walk in her shoes."

Of course, the problem with walking in her shoes is that you're still using your feet! You can say you understand and think you actually do understand her, but she may not be convinced. It's your job as a father to bend over backward to communicate that you truly want to know your daughter and understand her. This takes a great deal of energy, a willingness to hang in there when you feel like walking away, and a commitment to love your daughter enough to wade through layers of issues, feelings, and thoughts.

Sometimes this works itself out in the most mundane of circumstances, yet the little things add up to a lifetime of trust. Take, for instance, the following letter. This daughter shared the first thing that popped into her head when asked to write a letter to her dad:

> Dad,
> I want to thank you for not embarrassing me too much when I go on dates or bring someone over, even when you "accidentally" catch me kissing him. That's kind of embarrassing, but you don't say anything about it, until the next day when you tease me, for about five hours!
> —Meagan, 16, Columbus, OH

When your daughter thanks you for something as ordinary as how you treat her around her peers, it shows that she knows you not only care about her but you understand what she needs in those situations. As simple as that sounds, it has powerful implications for other areas of your relationship with her. Meagan obviously trusts her dad because she knows he understands her—at least a little bit.

When your daughter comes to the conclusion that she can trust you to work at knowing and understanding her, the groundwork for a lifetime of intimate and warm connection is created. This is the dream of every dad and the immense need of every daughter.

> Dear Dad,
> You have always made sure that I knew you loved me. And guess what? You are my number one hero. I talk about you all the time to my friends. I am so proud of you.
> —Mandy, 17, Tulsa, OK

When a daughter believes in her father and trusts him, her confidence is lifted, her sense of self is clear, and she learns how to trust herself. When she trusts herself, she can more freely trust others. Most important, she can more fully trust God. This is the ultimate goal of any father who truly loves his children — to create an atmosphere in which they will be able to trust in the One who created them.

# CHAPTER FOUR

# Closeness: The Adolescent Safety Net

*Dear Daddy,*

*I haven't been able to tell you this, but I've been scared lately. School was harder this year, and my friends don't seem the same. But I guess what scares me most is that I'm changing and I don't know what to do. I've always told you I would tell you everything, but we don't talk any more. I know it's mostly me, and I don't act like I want to talk, but I still need you, you know?*

*The speaker tonight talked about a poem a girl wrote called "Don't Be Fooled by Me." Don't be fooled by me, Dad. Please! I need to know that you are right beside me, even when I don't seem to care.*

—Cherie, 15, Boca Raton, FL

B eing "close" to someone is hard to describe and harder still to define, but we all want it with those we love. Closeness, although tied to expectations and attention, is defined more by a feeling than by something objective, measurable, or tangible. It's like a garden that must be looked after even though the gardener

Few girls in my town dated older guys, but I did. Now I have a pretty good understanding of what drove me to them. Once they paid attention to me, I was hooked!

I sometimes worried about dating an older guy. Our relationship was deep and very serious, almost from the beginning. So much of my world focused on him. Often, I made the choice to be with him at the expense of family and friends. I remember telling myself that I didn't have much of a choice, that love is costly. But I did feel strange about letting go of everyone and everything that I knew should be important to me—all for the sake of a guy.

Soon our "love" became a vicious circle. In my head I recognized that my relationship with him was excessive, to the point that other important relationships in

*(continued)*

realizes that growth is far beyond his control. The garden must be constantly tended through energy and focus. It doesn't matter to the wise gardener that the blossoms may not be realized until a future season. He recognizes that the fruit of his labor will eventually bring him the joy and beauty he seeks.

Throughout the early years of adolescence, every daughter is almost desperate to have a warm, close relationship with her father, but the struggle, the fighting, and the misunderstanding often cause her to deny what she craves. As the years progress, if her father is not responsive to what she wants and needs, she will look to other people—especially to other men—to fill the gap. For the father who realizes his daughter really does want a close relationship with him, the road to intimacy and depth is well marked.

The father who carefully plants, lovingly waters, and mercifully prunes—and who places his ultimate trust in his heavenly Father—will someday be close to his daughter. The roots of connection will be deeply embedded in the soil of the trust and intimacy he has built with her. Dad, your daughter wants to know you and love you. It is your task to allow her in.

Father-daughter closeness is a strange thing. In our research it was expressed by daughters in an either-or, black-or-white way. Either a daughter felt a closeness to her father and was grateful for it, or she felt distant from him, and along with it sadness and sometimes bitterness. These two letters are examples of the contrast we experienced.

> *Dear father,*
> *I'm tired of trying so hard only to be hurt. I'm not the perfect daughter. So what if my clothes are different? I just wish you would accept me as me. You have hurt me in so many ways yet I still try to love you. Can't you do the same?*
>
> —Brenda, 15, Charlotte, NC

> *Dear Dad,*
> *It may not seem like it sometimes, but I am so glad that God gave me you as my father. All my friends know what good friends we are, and I can tell they envy me! You are my biggest hero, you listen to me, you care about me, and I know I don't tell you often enough how much that means to me. I love you so much, and I am so glad that you are my dad!*
>
> —Cindy, 17, Baton Rouge, LA

These two letters flow from the same desire—a daughter's longing to be connected to her dad. The letter from Cindy doesn't mention specifically how close she

my life suffered. But emotionally I was consumed by him. I felt so right with him: He was there for me, he loved me, and I needed him. If I didn't see him for even one day I felt empty inside and longed to connect with passion and intimacy. I was barely sixteen.

Yet, even in the midst of adolescent passion, I sometimes wondered if the whole thing—the love, the depth, the longing—was right. Whenever I would get nervous, or scared, or even stop to think about my life, I would always come back to the single fact that this man loved me, and he proved it continually for three years. I needed his love, and without him I knew I would be lost. I had no one else. I felt like I needed a man in my life—a man who was kind, who listened, and who made sure I knew that I was valuable.

Dad, where were you when I needed you? What would you have said to me when I fell in love? Would I have fallen so hard had you blessed me, held me, loved me?

———

feels, but the tone of her letter describes a warmth and comfort that she experiences with her father. Brenda's letter, however, seems a desperate plea for acceptance. What she's really expressing is a desire to be close.

From the letters we've received, our experience with kids, and the latest social science research, it appears that, for most families, it's up to the father to determine the strength of the connection in his relationship with his daughter. If this is true, every father must ask himself (and perhaps even ask his daughter) one question: How close are we?

### The Role Fathers Play

During the past several decades of studies on the role of parents in the family, only a small handful of studies have focused specifically on fathers. Of those, the overwhelming majority were devoted exclusively to incestuous and abusive relationships. The father-child relationship is by far the most understudied of all human relationships, and fatherhood in general is the most understudied of all human roles. One research team reported that "a father was once popularly viewed as a distant, uninvolved role—a biological necessity, but a social accident, according to one famous definition."[1]

Perhaps this historically negative view of fatherhood has caused too little interest in the role a father plays. Yet all of us know that, for good or bad, our own fathers played a very important role in our lives. Only during the last few years have researchers started to take a serious look at the impact dads have on their kids. In seeking to understand how a father affects his children, researchers J. S. Turner and D. B. Helms summarized their findings this way:

> Until recently the role and impact of the father in child care has been overlooked. While the importance of the father in the household is generally recognized, part of

the problem is that American society has been "mother-centered" in its philosophy of child care. . . . [But current] research has clearly indicated that the father has strong influences on the child's overall emotional, social, and intellectual development. His presence and the attention that he directs toward his children has short- and long-term benefits. The absence of his care also seems to affect the development of the child.[2]

While the results are not yet conclusive, strong evidence suggests that a father's impact on his daughter during adolescence is far-reaching. A daughter's sense of self, for example, is usually connected to how she thinks her father sees her. If she feels that he thinks she is smart, she's far more likely to believe it herself. If she thinks he sees her as stupid or slow, the odds are strong that she will go through life believing it. While this is not universal, the majority of authentically confident women were raised by parents, and usually fathers, who constantly told them they were sharp and gifted leaders. A woman may achieve a sense of wholeness and health apart from the assurances of a committed, loving father, but she has a far better chance with one who cared about her as a young adolescent woman.

### The Nature of Father-Adolescent Daughter "Closeness"

The term associated with relational closeness in the family system is *attachment*. Attachment is defined as a feeling of closeness and intimacy with another person. Generally, attachment theory has focused on infants and their primary caretakers—usually mothers. But adolescent attachment is now understood as an important way to describe how close a young person feels to his or her parents (and peers). The strategic relational concept of adolescent attachment is gaining strength as one of the most important factors in an adolescent's development.

What is important for fathers to know is that attachment

seems to matter more than any other developmental character-istic in the father-adolescent relationship. When trying to under-stand how close or attached a father-adolescent relationship is, social scientists measure the adolescent's *perception* of how close he or she feels to the father. Why not measure the father's per-ception of the attachment in the relationship? Researchers have discovered that it doesn't make any measurable difference what a father may believe, or even what an independent observer believes, about the relationship. The only thing that matters in the long run for the child's development is how *the adolescent feels* about the relationship. If she feels close to her father, the relationship is considered close or highly attached. If she feels distant from her father, the relationship is seen to be distant or detached.

Attachment is different for adolescents than for infants. Obviously, there's no way to measure the sense of attachment in infants until they are old enough to talk about feelings and per-ceptions. In infant attachment research, a set of inferences is derived by trained observers of the relationship. It is an inexact method of research at best. For adolescents, the idea of attach-ment comes from how an adolescent *feels* about a given rela-tionship, regardless of what others see or experience. For adolescents, it is not the actual attachment that is being mea-sured but rather their *perception* of the feelings around attach-ment. Adolescent attachment is a far more accurate and helpful notion for understanding a young person's view of life and how he or she will live. If, for example, a father thinks he is fairly close to his daughter, but the daughter feels that they are actu-ally very distant, the daughter will live her life as disconnected from her dad. This in turn could cause her great pain as she moves through adolescence. Conversely, Dad may feel like he's failing miserably with his daughter. Yet, if *she* believes they are close, she will experience life as one set free by the perceived security of a close attachment relationship with her dad.

Adolescent attachment is not some lofty theory without any grounding in reality. Many researchers are concluding that the most important factor in how a child will respond to life's circumstances is the perception she carries of her attachment to her parents, and more specifically, to her father. Even those developmentalists who have virtually ignored adolescent attachment are beginning to recognize this growing body of evidence. As leading developmental author and educator John Santrock notes:

> Adolescents who were securely attached to parents also were securely attached to peers; those who were insecurely attached to parents were more likely to be insecurely attached to peers. And in another investigation, college students who were securely attached to their parents as children were more likely to have securely attached relationships with friends, dates, and spouses than their insecurely attached counterparts.[3]

*Daddy,*

*I was just writing you 'cause I was thinking about you. I have been doing it a lot lately. I have so many things to ask and say. I always wonder why you don't love me or want to be around me. What could I have done in my sixteen years to make you hate me? It really hurts me deep inside and always will. It affects me every day of my life and will for the rest of it. I pray that one day we could be like all of the other girls and dads I see. I feel so left out.*

*P.S. I'll always love you, no matter what.*

—Lisa, 16, Orlando, FL

For daughters, the feeling of closeness or attachment to their fathers is extremely important to their growth as women. These maturing women want and need to make a clear break from the bonds and roles of childhood. Every daughter must be set free to grow up, to experience life on her own, and to develop a personal sense of autonomy and identity.

For a daughter to break free from seeing herself as a child, she deeply desires and intuitively knows that she needs a close, warm, and intimate relationship with both her mother and her father. As she grows into adolescence, she no longer experiences her mother as a primary nurturer and caretaker; she desires to relate to her as a friend. This process takes several years and is not without struggle until they are both able to first recognize and then handle this switch in roles.

This is the time when a daughter's father plays such an important role in her life. He is the one she needs to form an attachment with while she begins to shift roles with her mother. She knows she must separate from Mom, for to become a woman she needs to see herself as a woman distinct from her mother. But she also knows that she cannot venture too far out there on her own as she takes those baby steps into adulthood. Adolescence is a time of *transition,* and a daughter needs her dad to catch her when she falls and to encourage her to keep moving ahead on this perilous yet exhilarating journey.

Because the power of father–adolescent daughter attachment is a relatively new concept, it is rarely addressed in books and articles. A few child development experts, however, have observed the process of shifting attachment needs from the mother to the father. Carol Gilligan, for example, who specializes in young women's development, describes this process:

> For women, the developmental markers of separation (from mother) and attachment (to father), allocated sequentially to adolescence and adulthood, seem in some sense to be fused . . . [but this is] currently obscured in psychological texts.[4]

Of course, both adolescent boys and girls need and desire to break off from the dependent relationship they had with their moms and develop more mature strong attachment relationships with their fathers. Boys have the same need of father attachment as do girls, but how they express and describe their need, how they see their fathers fulfilling their desires, and how they ultimately experience this attachment is very different from girls, at least in North American culture.

Researchers have observed two general differences between a boy's understanding of his father-attachment needs and a girl's understanding of the same. First, a girl is more in tune with what she wants from the relationship. Second, a girl is more aware of what is actually going on in the relationship.

An in-depth analysis into adolescent girls' needs is found in the book *Meeting at the Crossroads: The Landmark Book About the Turning Points in Girls' and Women's Lives*. This study discovered that a widespread trait of adolescent girls is the ability to intuitively perceive complex relational dynamics and alter their behavior accordingly: "Girls talk about the importance of paying close attention, of observing carefully, in determining the existence or extent of another person's pain."[5]

In our culture, girls talk more than boys do about relationships. They allow themselves to feel more in relationships than do boys, and they thoughtfully consider their own relational needs more than their male counterparts do. A son may want to be closer to his dad, but when he and his dad throw a ball around, he is generally somewhat satisfied. For a boy, in most cases, time spent together is usually all that matters.

For a girl, relational activities are a means to an end. She wants the emotional intimacy that comes with closeness and attachment, and so she will gladly participate in activities that she hopes will serve to deepen her relationship with her father. But she will not be satisfied until an intimate connection is established and growing.

Studies are just now being done to continue the quest to probe the depths of these understudied, mysterious, and highly complex relationships. But the early indications on the father–adolescent daughter relationship are overwhelming: This relationship is powerful, important, and has long-lasting impact on developing adolescents.

Do fathers desire a warm, intimate relationship with their daughters? Undoubtedly. Do daughters desire the same? Absolutely! What, then, must a father do to prove to his daughter that he, too, desires to connect with her? First, we'll look at obstacles to a close relationship and then explore four ways to make it happen.

## *Obstacles to Father–Adolescent Daughter Attachment*

### *Your Own History*

Few fathers in today's culture have seen models of what it means to attach to a daughter. The fathers who were raised from the 1950s until the 1970s experienced a cultural understanding of fatherhood in which men were seen as benevolent advice-givers who basically left the parenting role to the mothers. Naturally, exceptions abound. But in our society, few men have been taught what it means to parent a daughter. Even today, men's organizations are calling fathers to the importance of being nurturing parents, but the focus remains on being a good father to *sons*. Virtually no one is talking about how a father can (and must) invest in his daughter.

The important thing for you and your daughter to consider is the impact of your own history on the way you see the father role. What kind of models have you seen? Did you grow up with a warm, relational, and nurturing father who enjoyed close relationships with his children? Or was your father distant, unconnected, and removed from the family's daily affairs? The odds are great that you will relate to your kids in the same way your father related to you. You can work to break the trend, but the older you get, the more you will hear your dad's voice coming out of you as you interact with your own family.

Specifically, when it comes to being a dad to your daughter, how your own father treated your sisters and/or how he honored, respected, and valued your mother has planted seeds of behavior deep inside you that cannot help but come out as you deal with your own daughter. Many fathers want to be different from their dads, yet they are held back by powerful unseen forces that cause them to maintain multigenerational patterns of neglect and distance. The best antidote to a poor model of father-attachment is to take a close look at your family history and commit to working through the patterns and voices that keep you from caring for your daughter in the way she needs and deserves.

In other words, does your history and experience keep you from developing a close and attached relationship with your daughter? She's growing up and she needs you, Dad.

### Leaving It Up to Her

"If or when she needs me, she knows I'll always be there for her. All she's got to do is ask." This can be called the "parenting by default" method of raising daughters. But it's clear that unless a father proactively decides that he's going to cultivate an intimate relationship with his adolescent daughter and reaches out to her, it will not happen.

> *Dear Jerk (remember when you called me that?),*
> *Remember when you said it was up to us (kids) if we*
> *wanted to have a relationship with you? Well, let me tell*
> *you now that is the biggest bunch of bull I've ever heard!*
> —May, 15, Dallas, TX

### Being Unavailable

The demands of our hectic world are overwhelming. It's almost a cliché to say that. But it's so true that it's often hard for fathers to remember just what is important as they go through each day.

The years with your daughter are few and precious. She needs you to be around and to keep her on the "front burner" of your schedule. It's easy to forget how deeply our children long to connect with us and even easier to forget how much they *need* to connect with us. But we must be diligent and disciplined, or we will miss the opportunity to love our daughters into adulthood.

> Dear Dad,
> Some nights I would stay up crying until 3:00 A.M. when you were gone on a trip, wishing you would come and comfort me and say it was all right. You never did.
> P.S. I can't wait until you are home for good!
>
> —Virginia, 11, Kansas City

### Fear

There's no question that the biggest obstacle fathers face in attaching to their daughters is summed up in one word: fear. What do I *say*? How do I *act*? What happens when we argue and fight? How do I know the balance between tough love and discipline, between compassion and forgiveness?

In addition to the nuts-and-bolts, everyday issues fathers face, there lurks the broader and more complex dynamic of what happens when your daughter's body changes from Shirley Temple to Cheryl Ladd. As the inevitability of physiological change begins to affect how a daughter looks, moves, and dresses, most fathers are caught off guard, and many are uncomfortable. No longer does it "feel right" to give your daughter that bear hug or bounce her on your knee. She seems more like a woman and less like a little girl, and this can change how you feel and think about her. It also can change how you treat her. Yet it's vital for you to remember that even with a seventeen-year-old body, she is still your twelve-year-old daughter! And as she changes, she needs you more than ever. Letting these changes sneak up on you is forgivable. But letting these changes drive you away from her is relational suicide, for both you and her.

## Making It Happen

Your daughter wants you to attach to her, but she will probably wait for you to take the initiative. As an adolescent girl, it's likely that she's quite intuitive relationally, and she needs to know that you truly want to be close to her. She also needs to know that you are willing to do what it takes to be close to her before she will open up to a highly attached relationship. This is a process that can take many months or even years to achieve, depending on how close your relationship has been during her growing up years. But every father can make it happen. It's possible to develop a deeply attached relationship with your adolescent daughter.

Unfortunately, father-daughter attachment does not occur through a specific set of techniques or follow-the-manual methodology. Building a close relationship with your daughter takes a new way of thinking. Let's look at four principles that will help create the framework for a father and his adolescent daughter to build a lifelong attachment bond.

### Knowing That It's Your Job

If your daughter knows you care enough about her to gently and carefully pursue her, even when she acts as though she doesn't want to be pursued, she will intuitively begin to trust you. And that is one of the key issues in healthy attachment. It's not a "constantly on her back" kind of pursuing, but rather the tender, subtle, and consistent way you show her that she matters to you.

*Dear Daddy,*

*I sometimes find it hard to say thank you, and I wonder if you know how much I love you and appreciate all you do for me. Thank you for all your words of wisdom and all of your guidance in my walk with the Lord. Thank you for listening to me cry about things that are so small but that hurt so much! Something that I never thanked you for—my knee surgery and making me call you when I get where I'm going. Thank you for loving Christ and praying for me every day. I admire you—you are the best daddy in the whole world.*

—Pooh Bear, 14, Glendale, CA

Don't leave it up to your daughter to come to you. Just like the parable of the Good Shepherd in Luke 15, let her know that you will always be out there seeking to care for her and connect with her, even when she runs away.

She does need space to develop a healthy sense of self apart from the family, as well as the room to begin to make her own choices and decisions. Knowing that it's your job to attach to her means that, as you allow her freedom to grow up and find her way, you are there—praying, listening, and caring every step of the way.

### Knowing What She Needs

Without considering her developmental processes and individual needs, a father could actually do more harm than good if he simply tries to "attach" to his daughter in his own way and in his own time. Remember, the idea of father-adolescent attachment matters *only from the perspective of the adolescent*. You,

Dad, are not the one who needs to obtain and experience the depth of relationship and attachment. Watch out for those signs and signals that tell you how she's feeling and what she's going through. Your task then, as we will discuss later, is to be a guide more than a boss, a friend more than a protector, and a teacher more than a judge.

### Using the Calendar

If you're like most American men, unless a priority gets put on your schedule, it won't get attention. The Stephen Covey revolution (*The 7 Habits of Highly Effective People*) was so simple in concept yet profound in impact. Essentially, this management and lifestyle guru has told millions of people about the value of ordering life around what is important. He's made a lot of money by cleverly stating the obvious in a way that sounds new and profound. How did this happen? Covey and other you-can-make-it-happen types touched a nerve inside people with the message: You know what's important and you want to live healthy, whole lives. Now, do it!

Most fathers who think about it know that they need and want to spend significant time with their adolescent daughters. But many don't know what they need to do with that time. That's why we've written this book — not as a superficial "how-to" manual, but as a catalyst for the desire that God has placed inside every caring parent's heart. As a dad, you were *created for intimate relationships* (despite what pop-psychologists say to the contrary). Your daughter is "flesh of your flesh" and she longs to connect with you as she enters the minefield of adolescence.

Now, take that inner desire and make the decision to change the way you live by opening up time to take walks with her, go to breakfast, write a note, watch a rainstorm, or talk on the phone. Learn how to "waste" time efficiently. Learn the art of listening to the silence of intimate relationship. Slow down, relax, and breathe in the joy of an attached relationship with your daughter.

### Trusting God's Call

God knows exactly what He's doing when He gives us children. A child is God's way of saying to us as parents, "Here's how precious you are to me. Your joy is but a meager taste of the pleasure I receive from loving you." The term *father* is a gift to allow us into the heart of God by pointing to the intimate and personal nature of the relationship He offers to each one of His children. And as He loves you, He also loves your daughter, far more than you do!

To parent in today's dark and lonely world is a frightening thought. Danger and evil seem to lurk in the shadows, waiting to devour anyone who ventures too far from the light. It's amazingly easy for even the heartiest of parents to be paralyzed with fear over the "What if . . ." questions when it comes to their kids. We must learn how to relax, let go, and trust in God's power, love, and sovereignty.

He allowed us the honor of loving this precious soul for a few short years. Our role as parents is not to make sure the road is clear and that our child will never stumble, fail, make a mistake, or disappoint us. Though we are His flawed and human children, God desires for us be the kind of father He is with us, trusting that He's firmly in command of the universe, which includes our daughters.

May God grant you the faith to trust Him and to love as He loves. Attach to your daughter, but never stand in the way of her attachment to the One who is her first and true love.

> Dear Dad,
> I don't think there is anyone on this earth who God could have picked to be a better father for me. I know He couldn't have. I just want you to know that no matter what, I love you. I will always love you, and I will never lose you, because I'll be up there in God's kingdom with you for eternity. You can count on it.
>
> —Sally Jo, 19, Nashville, TN

# CHAPTER FIVE

# Communication: The Heart of Father-Daughter Intimacy

Dear Dad,

*I love you very much but we don't spend a lot of time together. We are two totally different people. I wish we had more things in common. I love to play soccer and you love to hunt. I love to talk on the phone and you love to watch sports. I think that is why we fight so much. I would love to spend more time with you. I would love to be able to talk about my problems to you. I love you very much.*

—Brigette, 13, Grand Rapids, MI

Communication can be defined as "the art of being understood." Most children think their parents never listen to them; most parents think their children never talk! Parents often think they've communicated with their child when they have verbally (and, in their view, clearly) expressed their thoughts, wishes, or demands. To these parents, communication is the art of speaking logically, rationally, forcefully. But to a child, especially an adolescent, communication occurs when a parent is more concerned with seeing the child's point of view than with any sort of dialogue.

To most kids, the biggest problem with parent-child communication is that parents are so busy talking that they never listen. To most parents, the biggest problem with parent-child communication is that kids never seem to *want* to open up to them.

Perhaps this is among the most basic of all family problems and issues—a failure on both sides to realize that expressing one's view is only one component of the communication process. Other essential elements of the communication process involve tone of voice, timing of the discussion, eye contact, meaning of words and terms, body language, and the way the receiver experiences (or feels) the message. In short, parents and adolescents often misunderstand each other, and both usually blame the other for the ensuing conflict.

---

### From Dee
## Memories of an Adult Daughter

—

It took years of adult life—faith, marriage, and children—for me to be able to hold a conversation with my dad. All the years I was growing up I never really knew how to talk to him, and he really didn't know how to talk to me! We were like two strangers walking side by side on a crowded street. When I was with him, nothing was there!

Talking for me came easy, especially with those I loved—both men and women, guys and girls. As a teenager, I could spend hours talking to a friend on the phone or hanging out with some guys I knew (especially my boyfriend). But when it came to my dad, it felt like he just wanted the basic facts in three minutes or less. I found myself feeling like an item in his appointment book instead of someone he wanted to invest his time in.

We used to spend more time together when I was

*(continued)*

---

*Dear Dad,*

*I don't know why you don't want to talk to me. I've tried so many times, but when you are ready to talk, you only lecture. I want you to know what I think for once. You've told me my whole life what you think, and now it's my turn. Come on, Dad, I know you can talk to me without lecturing . . . you do it with [my brother]. Is it because I'm a girl that you don't want to talk to me?*

—MaryAnne, 17, San Diego, CA

John Gray, author of *Men Are from Mars, Women Are from Venus,* has made a fortune telling Americans that the difference between men and women is simple: They're from different planets! On Venus, according to this popular prophet, women love to talk. This is his explanation for the way women interact and why they seem to relate better with each other than with men.

On Mars, men live in caves, where they fight and struggle with each other, are aggressive and domineering, do not talk much, and flee relational depth. Men, therefore, are nearly incapable of being emotionally and relationally intimate. This philosophy states that because men do not like to talk, and because it is not natural for them, they have a hard time experiencing depth in relationships *simply because they are from another planet!* The result of this overly simplistic descriptive formula is that men are encouraged — indeed, given permission — to deny any need to emotionally and verbally connect with others in a meaningful way.

> little. But as a young woman we became virtual strangers. I remember wishing that we could go back to the way things were when I was a child. I wished we could be a family again and that I could know what it was like to have a dad who was there for me.
>
> I would wonder: *Does he ever think about me? Does he miss me as much as I miss him?* So many times, especially late at night, I wondered what it would be like to be friends with my dad — to talk and to listen. It's what I wanted all along. It's all I ever wanted from him.
>
> ———

In our culture, the majority of men do seem to live out this celestial description. But according to the Bible, both men and women are created in the image of God. Of course there are differences between men and women. And it's true that men as a group tend to be less verbal than women. But to first trivialize and then ultimately glorify a man's difficulty in intimate conversation is to rob him of the joy of experiencing relationships the way God intended.

As God's image bearers, both men and women possess a powerful and beautiful gift — communication — that gives them the unique ability to allow another person into the deepest part of themselves. Contrary to popular wisdom, sex is not the most intimate of human activities. The most sacred and vulnerable thing any of us can do is to share the intimacy of our thoughts with another person. Communication is what defines us as divine image bearers, and the willingness to participate meaningfully in an intimate verbal and nonverbal exchange is the greatest gift God has given to us in relationships.

We are most human when we are listening and talking, and men are endowed by God to be every bit as verbal as women. It is our cultural training, popular mythology, and socially reinforced stereotyping that holds men back from being fully themselves. As a father, the greatest gift you can offer the daughter you love is to connect with her at the deepest level through the hard work of intimate communication.

> *Dear Dad,*
> *I love you, but we don't talk like we should. I know you let me do stuff that Mom doesn't let me do, but we have to talk at least once a week. We love each other, so can we talk, please?*
> *I love you like crazy,*
>
> —Stephanie, 12, Lexington, KY

A father must learn how to communicate with his daughter if he's going to develop the kind of relationship that will launch her into healthy adulthood. He must learn to recognize which modes of communication best convey information and which cause her to rebel.

Your daughter knows this intuitively, for women in our society are much more in tune with this truth. What she doesn't yet know, however, is that you have been socialized to hide emotions, to avoid verbal intimacy, and to give a nod to any deep interaction with a kind of rhetorical "head fake." She's heard you proclaim your love for her, but when she hits adolescence she's waiting for you to show your love by spending time and energy in the fascinating world of verbal give-and-take. This is where she truly lives, and her desire is to share this place with you. But it's the rare father who has even approached his daughter in the sanctuary of her soul. Most dads don't even know it exists.[1]

What does it take to enter this holy place of intimate communication with your daughter? Here are six hints to help you leave Mars and enter the land of Venus:

- take time to talk
- become a world-class listener
- develop the art of asking questions
- tell her about what you feel as well as what you think
- constantly bless her
- remember that communication is more than mere words

These tips will enable even the coldest and most distant dad to break down the communication barrier that seeks to destroy his relationship with his adolescent daughter.

### Take Time to Talk

You cannot escape this axiom of relating to your daughter: It takes time to build your relationship with her.

Maybe you feel that you do spend a lot of time with your daughter. Perhaps you do things to support her, like going to her dance recital or watching her play a sport. While she may appreciate this attention, most likely she wants more from you. She wants you to invest in your relationship with her, to "waste" time with her.

Men in our culture have been trained to order and structure their lives in such a way that life is more a problem to be solved than a life to be lived. But your daughter knows better, and so do you. What is most important in life is relationship, especially with the people we love the most.

> *Dear Dad,*
> *I have become a young woman now, and I'd like to talk to you about some of the difficult times and the good times. What I really want to say is that in the future, I hope we can spend more time together.*
>
> —LouAnn, 13, Madisonville, KY

LouAnn knows what she wants from her dad. The tragedy is that she may not have felt comfortable telling him what she wrote to us.

Your daughter wants to take time to be with you. Do you really want to take time to be with her? Once you decide that you really do care, and you determine that she is, indeed, one of the highest priorities in your life, you're well on the way to truly connecting with her. Communication can only happen when you want to be there. You pave the way for the chance to talk and to listen.

### Become a World-Class Listener

> *Dad,*
> *I want to give you this [letter], but I don't think it's my place to tell you [these things]. And I'm not sure if you would listen. You've been a great encouragement to me, always admiring and giving me advice on how to go for my goals. But at the same time, you never seem to listen. You like to interrupt or tell me I'm wrong. Sometimes I feel that you love me but that you don't respect what I say because I'm a girl. When you always listen and respect my brother but not me, that's just how I feel.*
>
> —A. J., 16, St. Louis, MO

In all likelihood, A. J.'s father would be hurt if he were to read this letter (remember, the names and cities have been changed). He might think he's doing a great job of caring for his daughter. He must be aware that he's a "great encouragement" to her, and he may be feeling fairly confident in his abilities as a dad. But the troubling truth is that the older A. J. gets, the more she needs him to change his style. She needs him to talk less and listen more. In chapter three we talked about respect. The most important way to communicate respect is to learn how to listen.

Here's a little test to see from a daughter's perspective what kind of listener you are. Give yourself a 1 (terrible) to 5 (terrific) score for how your daughter would grade you on each question:

_____ 1. I like to get my father's point of view on things I'm concerned about.

_____ 2. I tell my father about my problems and troubles.

_____ 3. Talking over my problems with my father makes me feel good and safe.

_____ 4. When we discuss things, my father cares about my point of view.

_____ 5. If my father knows something is bothering me, he asks me about it.

_____ 6. My father can tell when I'm upset about something.

_____ 7. My father helps me to talk about my difficulties.

_____ 8. My father has his own problems, but I still don't mind telling him about mine.

This instrument records your perception of how well you communicate with your daughter. Add up the numbers you recorded and compare your final score with this table:

| | |
|---|---|
| 08 - 13 | Get a clue, Dad! |
| 14 - 20 | You've got some work ahead of you. |
| 21 - 27 | Not bad, but she still needs you to show you're willing to work at it. |
| 28 - 34 | Pretty good! But don't rest on your laurels; she |

needs your focused attention.

35 - 40   Way to go, Dad! You're there for her.

Remember, this is a test of *your perception* of how your daughter sees your communication. If you *really* want to know, ask her to take the same test. She may not feel free to be completely honest with you, but if you've worked hard to prove that you really want to know how you're doing, she'll give you some idea of what she thinks. Communication with your daughter is not so much how you feel, rather it is how she perceives your ability and willingness to listen to her.

### Develop the Art of Asking Questions

Good discussions rarely just happen with any teenager. The busyness of their lives; the constant demands placed on them; the shifting expectations of parents, teachers, and friends; and the ever present nagging thoughts about self-worth and identity all keep the mind and lifestyle of an adolescent preoccupied. It's a wonder our kids survive at all! Add to this the confusion of transitioning from childhood to adulthood, and you have a person dealing with incredible stress, living on the edge of a breakdown.

Some people think this description is a gross overstatement, and it may be for some kids who are temperamentally better suited to cope with life's demands. But for the majority of kids, we believe that life is a never-ending drag race—powerful engines at full bore, no time to stop and regroup—as they live on the edge of frenzied and dangerous exhilaration, never really knowing if they are winning or losing the race. It's not easy to get those who are feeling this way to sit down and focus long enough for a meaningful conversation. Fathers (and mothers) are the ones who must help their children slow down and experience an intimate, trusting connection with them.

We hate to be blunt, but it's a fact that most parents are terrible at drawing out their kids' thoughts. The questions parents ask are usually so obvious and directive that a child doesn't have to stop and think to answer them; or they're so obscure that they make little sense in the world of an adolescent. A question like, "Did you have a good time?" or "Did you have a good day at school?" may sound to an adult like a leading question. But it's all too easy to say "Yes," "No," or even to grunt a sophomoric noise in response.

A question like, "What's one thing at school that made you feel good today?" is more likely to help your daughter reflect on something positive and then express it to you. Even better is a question like, "What's the worst thing about the worst teacher at school?" If she believes you really want to know, and you won't criticize her response, she'll easily become engaged in the conversation.

It's not just the *wording* of the question that makes a difference, it's the *timing* as well. A question asked over a Coke or while taking a walk — a question that drew little response the night before — could initiate a conversation that lasts through the dinner hour.

As you attempt to become a world-class listener, remember that your daughter may be carrying all kinds of burdens that even she may not understand. Sometimes the best way to listen is simply to ask to sit with her for a few minutes and talk about your day — not the "work" part but the "heart" part. If she seems interested, and you sense her readiness to respond, then turn the conversation around so that she feels safe and comfortable enough to open up.

### Tell Her What You Feel, Not Just What You Think

Most contemporary men think in terms of problems and solutions. At work this mindset is even more pronounced. But this isn't what your daughter wants or even needs to hear from you. She's far more interested in how you *feel* about any given situation or circumstance. This may be the toughest part of the father-daughter relationship—that your daughter is probably not the slightest bit interested in the mechanical or corporate struggles you have at work. She will at best feign interest whenever you drift to the business aspect of your day. But watch her perk up when you tell her how it felt when your boss criticized you for poor performance, or how hard it's been to watch the people in your company who have been laid off.

If you're honest, you know that you process these types of feelings every day. The trick is to have the courage to admit to your daughter the fear, loneliness, and insecurity you experience, even if you're tempted to think she won't understand or she won't be interested. She's far more interested in these things than in the business side of life or even her own activities and interests. She wants to know *you,* and she is intuitively capable of recognizing that you may try to hide behind the technical aspects of life. If she senses a defensiveness in you, or an unwillingness to allow her into your heart on this level, she will shut you out of hers.

> Dad,
> You've been an excellent dad, as much as you could. You have been through so much and learned so much wisdom but you just won't share it with me. You're always saying that your dad told you not to share your problems with your kids, but it's time to share your thoughts and beliefs. I'm really interested in what you've experienced and learned and believed. Tell me about you, Daddy. I really want to know you!
>
> —Samantha, 15, Charlotte, NC

### Constantly Bless Her

When Gary Smalley and John Trent wrote *The Blessing,* they reminded readers of an invaluable philosophy of parenting that many cultures have experienced for years. They describe the power that parents, and especially fathers, have in the lives and psyches of their kids by regularly offering the simple gift of a verbal affirmation. To bless our children is to hand them a lifelong gift of emotional, relational, familial, and spiritual rootedness. When we express to our kids how we believe in them as people, we help create an environment where their minds and hearts are shaped according to that blessing.

Henri Nouwen says that "to bless is *benedicere,* which means literally: saying good things."[2] The blessing you give your daughter is the gift of a "good word" that you proclaim to and for her. As these "good words" pile up and form layers of blessings within her soul, she will find herself surrounded by messages that will be a reminder of her unique beauty, her high standing before her family and God, and her ability to make an impact as she lives out who God has created her to be.

The letters we receive from daughters seem to fall neatly into one of two categories: those that reflect lives shaped by loving fathers who have spent years blessing their daughters, and those that reflect lives in which the blessing has been withheld. Indeed, the difference between a healthy father–daughter relationship and one in crisis is relative, constantly changing, and runs somewhere along a continuum between these two polarities. Those girls who tend to feel better about themselves seemed to express that their fathers had intentionally passed on scores of blessings through the years.

## Communication Is More Than Words

I am a very focused person. In fact, when I read, it takes a focused, all-out assault to interrupt me. It doesn't matter whether I'm reading the newspaper, a cheesy novel, or Calvin's *Institutes.* When I read, my mind goes into a trancelike state of concentration.

Enter my daughter, whom I love, as I read how the Colorado Rockies are the team to beat in the National League pennant race. She has been run over (literally) by one of her brothers (who happens to also be my son, but that's another book), and is in need of a sympathetic paternal ear and a focused fatherly heart. She comes into the kitchen and stands a few feet from where I sit, reading my paper, and doesn't make a sound (not counting, of course, the subtle yet discernible occasional whimpers of pain made more intense by the frustration of knowing I'm clueless). Of course I don't hear or notice her. Finally she speaks, "Dad! I've been standing here for five minutes!" I, being the fathering expert, momentarily glance up and say, "Oh, hi honey" and return to my morning's first love.

At this stage of our lives, my daughter still feels that I, while exasperatingly ignorant, am within some range of hope. Thus, she approaches the paper. "Dad, I need to talk to you!"

"Okay, honey, I'm almost done," I say, not looking up.

"DAD! I NEED TO TALK TO YOU—NOW!"

I finally get the message. And I am truly sorry, for I love my daughter and really want her to know that she's far more important to me than the sports section. (Now, for those fathers whose inner being is screaming, "I need my time, too," and "Sometimes it's good for kids to wait," I agree, to a point. But the sports page?)

This time it's too late. I've let her down. The moment has passed, and I've allowed my inability to focus to push her away.

With the crazy schedules we keep and the myriad pressures we all face as parents, our daughters are often left behind to wait for us to make room for their seemingly inconsequential interruptions. I want to be the kind of father who is willing, whenever possible, to be available to my daughter. There must be thoughtful balance, for children can take advantage of a parent who unthinkingly allows no personal space or boundaries. But that is rarely my problem. I am far more guilty of not focusing on her than I am of allowing her to invade my necessary boundaries.

How about you?

# CHAPTER SIX

# "Who Am I?"
# A Daughter's Search
# for Identity

*Dear Dad,*
*Last week when you asked me, "Who do you think you are,*
*young lady?" I had no answer for you. I was so mad and*
*frustrated and hurt that I wanted to scream and cry,*
*but all I did was stare at you, then I turned and walked*
*away. I wanted to say, "Do you know who I am?" I'm your*
*daughter, and if you don't know who I am, who does?*
*Then, when the words weren't there, I wanted to tell you*
*that I have no idea who I am! But I couldn't tell you any*
*of this. I was mad, you were mad, and we never talked*
*about it. Now that I think about it, I really wish I knew*
*who I am. And I really wish that you knew who I am.*

—Sarah, 15, Georgia

"Who do you think you are?"

This worn-out query is most often spoken on an exhale of frustration. But what a question to ask a daughter in the throes of adolescence! In her seemingly endless search for a clear sense of self, a fifteen-year-old girl cannot hope to satisfactorily

## From Dee
### Memories of an Adult Daughter

―――

When I was growing up, the world was a strange and cruel place. It seemed to shout so many messages at me:

- I had to be thin, fit, and confident to be popular.
- I needed to get a good education to succeed in life.
- I needed to stand tall as a woman and to forge new career trails for future women in the American workplace.
- I needed to be married and have children in order to be complete as a woman.
- I needed to be involved in the church, giving myself away to others, even before I knew for sure who that "self" was!

Every girl faces a similar list of expectations, voices, and opinions, and usually they are as subtle as they are powerful. They felt so overwhelming to me at times that I just wanted to give in, remain a kid, and avoid the whole adult thing all together.

―――

respond to such a question. What is she supposed to say? Most girls at this stage of development are desperately trying to find out for themselves.

Much discussion has taken place lately over the exact meaning of the concept of *identity*. Some claim that it is our sense of self as we relate to others or to the roles we play. Others refer to identity as specific areas of behavior or lifestyle, such as sexual or familial identity. Still others seek to describe who we see ourselves to be underneath our behavior and beyond our self-expression. One thing is certain, Dad: Your adolescent daughter is on a quest to discover who she is, and she wants your help.

Sarah's letter reflects this key struggle in the life of every adolescent. The technical name for it is *individuation*. Basically, it is the process of becoming an adult. Contrary to much popular thought, the process of individuation does not mean that your daughter wishes to make a clean break from you and your family. It simply means that she wants (and needs) to become her own person within the context of your family. This is the essence of the adolescent journey—moving from being a child who is defined by her family to functioning as an independent adult member of the family system.

There are two aspects of individuation: the formation of personal identity ("Who am I?") and the development of personal autonomy ("My choices matter!"). This chapter deals with the first issue, identity. We'll talk about autonomy in chapter seven.

### Marcia's Story

Marcia is sixteen. She's outgoing, polite, and very smart. She plays the piano, is a star soccer player, and has several guys wanting her to notice them. She appears confident and self-assured. She can look you in the eye and smile with genuine warmth each time she talks to you. Anyone who has been around her feels as though she's as solid a kid as they come. She's spent a lifetime making sure people in her life believe that. But there's more to Marcia's story.

When she was twelve, Marcia's parents went through a difficult time. Her dad left home for a few months "to think about what I need," he told Marcia. The day he left he told her, as the eldest of four kids, "I need you to take care of your brothers and sisters, Marcia. Your mom and I are going through a rough time right now, and she won't be much help. I need to live my own life for a while, so I need you to make sure that everybody is okay. I'm counting on you to be grown up. I know you won't let me down." With that, he turned and walked out the door.

During the next several months, Marcia's father came home to visit a few times, but he was virtually out of their lives. Those rare times when he did return, he talked to her mother and played with her little brothers and baby sister. Marcia was tall for her age and had developed to the point that she looked many years older. Her dad didn't seem to know how to react to her. He continued to admonish her to "keep holding the family together" and told her that he was proud of "how well you are doing." Yet he seemed distant from Marcia's perspective. She felt that he never wanted to talk to her and didn't seem to care what *she* was needing or how much she needed someone to watch out for *her.* She was forced to play a role — the mature, confident, self-assured, stable member of the family.

By now she was fourteen, a young woman growing up with the burden of having to be all things to all people but not having any idea who or what she was inside. No one had allowed her to take the time to figure out just who was hiding beneath that calm and cool exterior.

I met Marcia when I was speaking at a youth conference. I had mentioned during one message that often we try to find our identity in what we do, what we control, and what others say about us.[1] I went on to share that God has created each of us with a smile, and that each person is a precious masterpiece personally sculpted by the hand of the loving Creator.

Marcia was cautious as she approached me, but it was obvious that she wanted to talk. As she told me her story, I saw her countenance change from that of a confident student-athlete to a lost young woman. While she had become adept at creating and then living out a variety of roles, she had lost her sense of self somewhere along the way. She was lost in a family system that forced her to play responsible roles at the expense of exploring who she was. Although she was still young, the years had taken their toll on her and she was deeply wounded.

As she walked away, I couldn't shake the feeling that Marcia's journey will be a long and lonely one for years to come. But at least she had come to realize that she must allow herself to begin the process of finding herself.

## Helping Your Daughter in Her Search for Identity

Although we hear much talk today about "sexual identity" and "gender identity," there is much more to your daughter's need to develop her own sense of personal identity.

Much of what a girl discovers about what it means to be a woman is in the modeling and attachment she receives from her mother (and other women). But true growth into womanhood needs to be much more about character, giftedness, passion, and heart than how a young woman lives out her "gender role." This is the gift a father can give his daughter. He can help her to discover and then celebrate the person God sees her to be.

Your daughter was created from the heart of the heavenly Father, knit together by the hand of the Son. By the Spirit, she has been stamped forever with God's image. As she strives to answer the question, "Who am I?", your daughter must continually be reminded that at the core of her being she is God's special child, dearly loved and created for a unique purpose.

A father's role in this process is to help his daughter see that she is already a unique and precious child of God. The search for her identity is more about discovering *who she already is* than about becoming something or someone else.

> ### From Dee
> ### Memories of an Adult Daughter
>
> ---
>
> There were times when I really missed having a dad around. I felt that I was on my own, trying to figure out who I was in the midst of the chaos. Somehow I had to filter through all those voices screaming at me and discover my own identity. I wonder how those years would have been different if I'd had a dad who loved me, talked with me, and blessed me as I grew up?
>
> ---

An old African proverb says, "There is a Dream dreaming us." Author Robert Benson takes this idea further by stating that many people today are "lost somewhere between the dreaming and the coming true."[2] This phrase is especially true for so many young people today. God is thinking about your daughter even as you read this. He has a plan for her — a "dream." Yet, if she's like most kids, she has no idea that she is that precious to the One who created her. Your daughter needs to know that she doesn't have to go on a search for her identity. It is readily available through a relationship with the One who made her. As Augustine said, "My soul was restless until I found my rest in Thee." You need to help her see that we discover who we are when we surrender to the love and chosenness of God.

## A Historical Look at Identity

Developmentalist Erik Erikson, writing in 1950, described male identity as being built in terms of experience with the world. In contrast, he said that female identity is determined through relational intimacy. According to modern developmentalists, however, the latest research claims that "there are now fewer gender differences in identity than the earlier studies suggested."[3]

Both adolescent girls and boys need to discover who they are through relational intimacy *and* life experience. Throughout the history of developmental theory, it has been assumed that parents play some sort of role. But little attention has been given to this piece of the puzzle. Until just a few years ago, fathers were essentially excluded from the developmental formula. Social scientists now acknowledge that both mothers and fathers "are important figures in the adolescent's development of identity."[4] When placed alongside the research on father attachment, it's clear that during a child's quest for healthy identity formation, both the mother and the father are vital participants in the growing-up process.

Erikson's view that boys and girls discover their identities differently have largely gone unchallenged, even today. Therapist Patricia H. Davis does, however, make a distinction between Erikson's theory and modern views on adolescent girls' development in her book *Counseling Adolescent Girls*:

> Developmental psychologist Erik Erikson describes the ways in which both adolescent boys and girls work to find their own identities in his idea of the "identity crisis." For boys, Erikson's process describes the whole struggle; for most girls, Erikson's theory describes half of what she must accomplish. The second half of a girl's process of identity formation is described by Carol Gilligan; it is the process of coming to 'truth' about the self and how the self negotiates relationships. . . . For

girls this process of forming an identity often involves tricky negotiations. Not too many years ago . . . a girl's options were so few that the question of her adult identity was settled almost as soon as she reached puberty.[5]

While Davis falls into the secular trap of seeing identity solely in terms of roles, she does acknowledge that adolescent girls need a greater degree of sensitivity as they grow up. In terms of the roles women have been encouraged to fill as they flesh out their identity, women's roles today are much more open than even ten years ago. A girl's identity is no longer defined solely by the traditional roles of marriage and motherhood. This is now causing a crisis of sorts in adolescent girls as they seek the answers to the questions "Who am I?" "What do I do with my life, and how do I know?"

In our society girls are explicitly taught that they have both the right and the cultural power to choose their own identity and to create the roles they desire to live out. Implicitly, especially in the church, most girls are expected to go to college and prepare for the future, but always with an eye on finding fulfillment in marriage and in marital and maternal roles. Depending on your church, this message ranges from a subtle suggestion that nags at your daughter internally to an overt statement that reinforces a cultural stereotype no longer existing in our society.

There are still people and churches who teach that women are fully complete only when and if they get married. That teaching leads to a woman's primary identity being found exclusively within the context of that role. How does your daughter navigate such confusing waters? Who is right?

Messages, whether subtle or overt, that tell a young woman who she is by what role she takes on, often cause a struggle within the young woman who is seeking to discover who she is and how she fits in the world. The question is not a matter of "biblical roles," for the culture is so dramatically different today than it was during the life of Jesus and Paul. Some may long for "the good old days," when roles were clear and everyone knew what was expected of them. But this type of thinking will not be able to withstand the tide of cultural change. The current is too strong, and the waves are too powerful for the church to define for young women who they are to be and what specific roles they are to play.

In the meantime, as Christians debate over a woman's role in society, the church, and even the household, adolescent girls are being swept away, lost, insecure, without a place to land. Your daughter needs help as she attempts to discover who she is and how she is to order her life—all within a world that doesn't seem to care very much.

## *A Father's Role—Seeing Her as Unique*

Daughters in today's world need mothers and fathers who are willing to trust God's creative handiwork when it comes to their identities. Society cannot dictate who your daughter is to be, nor is the church called to handle the task. Instead, a daughter needs a few select people in her life who have the conviction and ability to help her become *the person God created her to be!*

During the adolescent journey, a father has a unique opportunity to influence his daughter one way or the other. If he's stuck in the mire of philosophical and pseudo-psychological debate raging over "a woman's place," he may cause her to deny who she is simply to please him. God may have created her with unique and powerful gifts for furthering His kingdom, but this kind of father may also ignore his daughter's natural giftedness and push her into prescribed roles and relationships that can snuff out the creative spark offered her in the miracle of the way God created her.

On the other hand, a father who believes that God knew exactly what He was doing when He created his daughter waits expectantly to see the gift of God as she emerges from the cocoon of adolescence. That is the real joy of parenting—the wonder of seeing your child show signs of the beautiful majesty of God's creation as she discovers who she is in Christ! A father who is willing to love and willing to wait on the Lord; a father who is willing to trust that who his daughter has been created to be, is far better than what she is culturally predetermined to be will receive the reward he desires—a daughter who knows her God and who knows and likes herself.

The following letter came from a daughter whose father seemed to be more concerned with her fitting into cultural expectations than in allowing her to discover her created self.

Dear Dad,

I know you are disappointed in me, but I've been living a lie for many years, and I can't any longer. I don't know how to tell you this, and it's easier to write you than to talk to you, but I have decided that I'm breaking up with [my boyfriend] and dropping out of school [a Christian college]. I've been trying so hard to be the perfect little Christian daughter, and trying to be everything you ever wanted me to be, but I just can't anymore. I don't know who I am or what I want! I don't want to hurt you, but I have been hurting myself for so long, and I have to stop, now!

Dad, I'm still a Christian (you don't have to worry about that), but I don't know if my relationship to God is the same as your relationship to God. I want to follow Jesus, and I want to give my life to Him, but I also want to find out who I am, too! Please try to understand, and don't hate me. I still love you. I will always love you.

—Carol, 20, Salem, OR

The struggle in Carol's letter is obvious. We don't know if she ever gave her dad a similar letter or if she ever told him what she felt. One thing we do know: Carol loves her dad very much. And she feels like she's breaking his heart as she tries to figure out who she is and what she wants and needs out of life. The God she had grown to love, follow, and worship had not seemed the same to her as the God she was raised with. In discovering herself, Carol was also seeking to discover her faith. In the process, she felt that she needed to break away from the suffocating control of her father. He may be a gentle, loving man of God. But her perception of how he controlled her decisions and life made her feel as if she was denying who she was. The journey has been a hard one for Carol. Unfortunately, what she needed from her dad was encouragement in the process instead of a predetermined dictation of who he wanted her to be.

As developmental theorist Carol Gilligan writes:

> Developmental psychologists who are sensitive to the differences between girls and boys as they enter puberty and young adulthood are discovering that this time is often particularly difficult for the girls. Researchers find that in early adolescence, especially, girls are prone to depression and to losing hold of their precious newly emerged identities. This is not surprising in a culture that misunderstands and ignores their perceptions and visions, but is eager to exploit them for financial and other unethical gain.[6]

Harsh words, but a great deal of research supports Gilligan's position. Adolescence is a fragile time for your daughter. In a sea of strange, frightening, and wonderful emotional and physical changes, she is desperately trying to land somewhere safe and solid. She needs to know who she is and how she fits in this rapidly shifting world.

### The Comparison Game

As she tries on various roles and pseudo-identities, it will be hard for your daughter not to become adept at the comparison game, measuring herself against everyone and everything.

Some theorists argue that such comparison is a healthy path to discovering identity because it differentiates who we are—our strengths and weakness, our gifts and talents, and our individual personalities and temperaments—from those around us. But common sense seems to scream out just the opposite. In comparing ourselves to others, we become equipped to identify differences, but our natural response to these differences is to see ourselves as lesser than those we are comparing ourselves to!

When we live by comparison, we constantly reinforce our inner conviction that we are not who we want to be. Therefore, we see ourselves as incapable and insignificant in the grand scheme of things. These seeds are sown during adolescence, and this tendency appears to be more pronounced in girls than in boys.

The game doesn't end at adolescence; many adult women continue to suffer from the comparison syndrome. A daughter needs to be told early on that she need not compare herself to others, because she is a valuable, gifted, talented person in her own right.

Mike Yaconelli, owner of Youth Specialties, once told an audience, "I've always thought that when I got to heaven, God would say to me, 'Mike, I'm glad you're here. But, Mike, why weren't you more like Moses? I liked Moses. He was *really* a servant of mine.' But I've only recently come to see that the greatest struggle for me has been to try and live as me! I am now beginning to see that God is more likely to say to me, 'Mike! Welcome, Mike. And, Mike, why weren't you *Mike?*'"

On paper it seems so obvious, almost trite. Yet in your daughter's daily struggle to find her own sense of identity, it's so hard for her simply to be herself. She barely knows who that is. She needs to be reminded that she's the person who hides alone inside her heart. That person has been created by God to soar as one set free to be completely herself.

## A Father's Message

We have a ritual in the mornings at our house. When our kids head out the door for the day, we have a message for each one of them. I say, as each one leaves, "Let the Lord love you, and use that love to love others." Dee then offers this daily reminder: "Remember who you are. And, I love you." Our kids tend to respond with an "Okay" as they walk out the door. It's not a tightly controlled ritual, but it is a daily goal for us.

We know that we don't have the power to force our children to "let the Lord love them" or to "remember who they are." And rituals like this can turn into sappy, meaningless grunts if we're not careful. But we want our kids to go through adolescence being reminded every day that who they are and what they have to offer in the world comes from God, who loves them. We are His channels of that love or, as Philip Yancey writes, His "dispensers of grace." We pray that our lives reflect our words, and also that our children will experience the truth behind the words as they try to discover for themselves who they are.

As parents, and especially as fathers, the words we speak can be a potent reservoir of healing and empowerment. May the teaching of our Lord's best friend on earth spur us on to be good and wise stewards of what we say to our children:

> If anyone speaks, he should do it as one speaking the very words of God. If anyone serves, he should do it with the strength God provides, so that in all things God may be praised through Jesus Christ. To him be the glory and the power for ever and ever. Amen. (1 Peter 4:11)

Tell your daughter that she is loved—tell her every day. Remind her that God has made her beautiful, wonderful, and gifted. She is a masterpiece of the living God, and you get to be the messenger of that wild, wonderful truth!

# CHAPTER SEVEN

# Letting Go:
# Helping Her
# Become Autonomous

*Dear Dad,*
*I know it makes you sad to see me grow up, but when are*
*you going to realize that I'm not eight years old*
*anymore?! I love you, but you can't seem to understand*
*that your "precious little baby" is gone forever!*

Pam, 17, Orlando, FL

Every daughter is one of a kind. Child developmentalists, family researchers, and therapists all agree that when everything is said and done, every human being is absolutely and completely unique. And because no two children will ever be the same, each child brings to the world a brand-new mix of complex feelings, abilities, temperament, and responsive inclinations.

This great weakness of social science is rarely admitted. Yet, to codify, predict, or even to describe accurately what goes on in an individual's heart, soul, and mind—or how he or she is going to respond to a given set of circumstances—is extremely unlikely if not virtually impossible because no two people are

(continued)

*From Dee*

**Memories of an Adult Daughter**

Growing up without a dad around, I can remember feeling as though I didn't have a protector. I was vulnerable to the world around me. I felt like I needed to learn how to take care of myself, stand on my own two feet, be independent and strong. As a result, I broke away from my mom and sister much earlier than I was ready. Although I felt a drive toward independence that I thought I could handle, in reality I lacked the maturity and experience to make healthy or smart decisions. No one could tell me differently, however, for I was on a quest to prove to the world that I was mature and capable.

In hindsight, I realize this push for independence was a defensive reaction to the very thing I needed and longed for the most — the loving safety of a father's arms that were big enough to hold me through the con-

alike. God built this gift into us when he created humanity: Every life brings a fresh picture of the creative touch of the Master Artist. No one will ever be the same as someone else.

Oh, sure, genetics play a role in what our kids are like, as does environment. But two kids from the same parents in the same house will often turn out to be different in just about every way. This is especially true when it comes to boys and girls. Gender may not be the key issue in terms of how kids experience and report sibling differences within the family, but to many adolescent girls, it sure feels that way.

*Dear Dad,*

*Don't you know that I need you as much as Ricky? Do you think he is the only one who wants to be with you? You say that you want to be with me, but when I try to talk to you, you just tell me what to do. Ricky got to get his permit when he was old enough, but I'm almost sixteen and you say I'm not ready! Ricky can stay out late with his friends, but you say you "don't know my friends." C'mon, Dad, wake up! You give Ricky so much more freedom than you give me, and yet you still won't talk to me about it!*

—Sandra, almost 16, Denver, CO

Sandra's complaint is but a symptom of the core issue of her adolescent struggle — the perception she carries of her father's comparison of her with her brother Ricky. She believes that she's treated differently just because she's a girl and that triggers all kinds of emotions within her. Over time, this can foster an unstable sense of self.

Her letter is more a plea for her father to love her than it is a complaint about her brother. She wants to be listened to and taken seriously. She wants her father not only to love her but to value her. When she observes the relationship her brother and father have, she sees no option but to draw a comparison. Sandra needs her father to recognize her uniqueness in a world that is constantly comparing her to others who are better looking, faster, "cooler," and smarter than she thinks she is. This is tied up with an even more basic need — that her father see her as strong enough to make at least some of her own decisions.

fusion and pain of transition. Arms that responded with love when I made mistakes. Arms that offered me strength and wisdom. Arms that could help prepare me for the vast world and still be there when I wanted to come running back. Deep inside I wanted and needed that safety in order to become the woman God designed me to be. Without it, though I was still young, I was forced to be independent, and to walk my own path through adolescence.

———

## The Search for Autonomy

The previous chapter detailed the first life task of an adolescent — the search for identity. Now we turn to the second life task of an adolescent daughter — the need to see her choices as making a difference. This has been called "developing an internal locus of control."

A sense of autonomy is rooted in a person's innate need and desire to stand tall through life as a unique individual. This need can only be fulfilled when it springs from a healthy sense of self. Identity and autonomy work together. Before a daughter can truly pursue a healthy sense of autonomy, she must first know who she is. Then she must believe in the person she sees herself to be.

Autonomy—the natural consequence of a healthy and growing identity—is not a battle for independence from family, even though it might look or feel that way. Certainly, your daughter may use words that sound like that's what she wants, and she may even seek such an arrangement. But a mature sense of autonomy is not simply a clean and total cut from those people who provide her with warmth, security, and love. It is the natural result of her need to become a fully functioning and equal member of those systems to which she is connected, especially of her family.

*Interdependence* is her real goal, not independence—a state in which she will ultimately feel isolated and alone. And the goal is not dependence—a state in which she feels less valued than others and ultimately a less important and less valued member of the system. No, she longs to discover herself as a gifted, unique person in her own right (identity), who is connected to the other members of the family while being able to function on her own by making some decisions and choices and then living with those choices. The truth is that your daughter cannot function without a belief that she has power over her life. While this may sound "worldly" to some Christians ("Isn't God in control?"), every healthy adult has at least some measure of personal autonomy. Without it, we would not have the confidence to get a job, obtain a mortgage, or get married.

The previous chapter dealt with a father's role in helping his daughter discover that her identity rests in her relationship to the heavenly Father. This chapter details what a father can do to help his daughter understand and experience autonomy. We will also discuss the difference between *identity* and *autonomy*. While they are related, identity—helping your daughter "find herself"—is much easier to help her achieve emotionally than helping her become autonomous. A daughter's search for autonomy is where a father's love, commitment, and concern are severely tested.

## Are You Ready to Let Go?

> Dear Daddy,
> I hope you won't be mad at me, but I need to tell you to back off (there's no other way I can say it). I love you, and you are the greatest dad in the world, but I am not a little girl anymore. You need to let me go. I used to think it was neat when you would say how you hate it that I was growing up, but now I don't think it is. I want you to know that, whether you like it or not, I am growing up, and I am becoming a woman. It's now up to me to decide what I do, what I wear, who I date, and how I spend my time. If you don't let me or try to stop me, I'll do it anyway. I don't mean to hurt you, but I'm almost eighteen and then I really am on my own (legally). So, Dad, please let me go!
>
> —Karen, 17, Minneapolis, MN

It doesn't cost a father much to help his daughter find her own sense of self. Yes, you may be nervous as she goes through the process. There will be moments and seasons of experimentation with clothes and friends, especially in middle or junior high school. Hairstyles and music may push you to the edge of panic. But all in all, these are manifestations of an inner process, and they are usually relatively harmless. Generally speaking, a loving father who invests wisely in his daughter will soon feel proud and satisfied by the emerging young woman he loves.

In the case of autonomy, the process (and everything related to it) is a much different experience. A daughter's quest for a healthy sense of personal autonomy deals with issues that cut to the core of a father's historical role in most families. Autonomy has to do with control, choice, and sometimes painful consequences.

From a practical point of view, autonomy is the most

common point of contention and dissatisfaction between a daughter and her father. Most daughters want more freedom than they are given, and most fathers want to put off the inevitability of their daughters growing up. The reality is that by the time a girl is eighteen, her father has very little control over her choices. The father who wants to be confident that his daughter will handle the complexity of everyday life must learn how to give her more and more room to experiment, and even fail, *while she is still under his control and authority!*

Unfortunately, there is no secret to making it through your daughter's search for autonomy. We would love to tell you about "Six Surefire, Painless Ways to Ensure That Your Daughter Will Become a Confident and Well-Adjusted Adult" (for only $99.99). As long as you live by a certain set of principles, your daughter will move from childhood to adulthood painlessly and with little turmoil in the family. We'd love to say that all a daughter needs is love and support from her parents to always make the right choices. Perhaps some philosophies and styles of parenting promise such hogwash, but the truth is that all such statements are lies.

The first idea, that there's a formula that will produce the kind of results you want for your daughter is not much more than wishful thinking. We live in an age of popular programs that promise everything from easy weight loss to financial security. But life is much more a fluid process with complex pieces than a simple formula that works for everyone.

Right now you may be saying, "Wait a minute, you've included lists (or tips) to put these concepts into practice." We're using the lists as *supportive information* to help flesh out the ideas presented. When someone claims that a program is all that's necessary for raising children, life becomes more of a paint-by-the-numbers, fill-in-the-blank game than a wild dance of faith.

Raising kids is a tremendous opportunity for faith, surprise, and trust. Raising a daughter—while nerve-racking and exhilarating at the same time—is an adventure. And because no two daughters are alike and no two fathers are alike, a paint-by-the-numbers approach just won't cut it.

Second, helping your daughter move from childhood to adulthood is not simply a commitment to live according to a set of principles. Living by principles is a good, *general* way to live, and certainly there are principles laid out in Scripture that are helpful in many life circumstances when raising a daughter. But the greatest problem with a set of principles is the way they often subtly shift from principle to law.

As your daughter passes through adolescence, the last thing she wants (or even needs) is perceived rigidity on the part of her parents. There is no specific, clear-cut time when a daughter is ready to drive, increase her curfew, or be allowed to date. To help your daughter move through this process, in terms of her personal autonomy, the authority you grant her as she makes certain choices must be handed off over time, based upon a variety of negotiated factors.

When a parent establishes and then commits to a series of principles from which to operate, a daughter may sense a noose around her neck. In this perceived constriction, she may do one of two things: She either will leave the home (physically or at least emotionally and relationally), or she will buckle under. The first is bad enough; for if she "checks out" of the family to make her own choices without the support, guidance, love, and forgiveness of her father, she may make even more destructive behavioral choices. But if she shuts down and allows a father to control her by a rigid set of "principles," someday she will find herself bitter and angry over her father's need to control her just when she was needing to understand the notion of freedom and decision making. When she realizes this, she will become angry and rebel. Most likely this will happen when she's long gone from the protective and nurturing shield of father attachment.

Third, some parents are so concerned with the appearance

of love that they abdicate their responsibility to help their daughter as she begins to unfold her "autonomy" wings. Loving your daughter doesn't mean letting her do whatever she wants, whenever she wants.

By the late middle school years, modern North American parents seem to have capitulated their responsibility of offering help, guidance, and discipline to their children. In the name of love, some kids stay up as late as they want, even on school nights. In the name of acceptance, some children have no curfew. In the name of relational harmony, many parents think that discipline ceases when a girl hits adolescence, and their role becomes that of a counselor when and if she ever seeks out a "counseling session."

*Love* is a wonderful, tender word that carries different expectations to different families and households. How we define a father's love will ultimately dictate how we help our daughters become autonomous while still maintaining enough order and constraint to keep her choices from doing major damage.

Helping your daughter walk the tightrope of adolescence while offering her the safety net of attachment is no simple task. We've found three basic areas that are crucial to the father-daughter relationship if a father is to help his daughter make wise choices and stand on her own. These areas are an ability to understand, a weaning process, and a warm embrace.

### Understanding

Researchers have discovered that as girls grow older they "seem to undergo a kind of crisis in response to adolescence and to the strictures and demands of the culture."[1] Although some parents (and especially fathers) may not recognize this, adolescence is a difficult process for most girls.

Historically, social scientists, educators, physicians, and even therapists have believed that the adolescent journey is roughly the same process for boys and girls. They have also believed that the process essentially described a child separating from her family. Many people who work with young people, even those who teach teachers, subscribe to this view. They continue to teach and counsel that it is healthy for young people to break ties with their parents and families. However, the simplistic nature of this view is dangerous, for it is observably accurate enough to appear true. However, over the last decade or so, social science has begun to affirm loudly that the opposite is true. The healthiest adolescent (or fledgling adult) is one who is intimately and joyfully connected to her parents and siblings.

Every father must be aware of a daughter's need for relational attachment to him during adolescence. As we have stated, and social scientists affirm, "healthy development throughout the adolescent period is a dual process of autonomy *and* family connectedness and attachment."[2] In other words, a developing sense of autonomy is not mutually exclusive with a need to be close to parents, and especially to a father. In fact, the reverse is true. A healthy sense of autonomy is more readily achieved and is an emotionally safer experience when a daughter feels connected to her dad. During and throughout adolescence the parental role shifts from authority figure to helping friend. This is why attachment is so crucial during this phase of development.

*Dear father,*
*I need you to know I need you.*

—Anonymous, Georgia

## A Weaning Process

Patricia H. Davis, in *Counseling Adolescent Girls,* notes that adolescents need to know that their feelings and needs matter to their fathers.

One of the most frequent complaints girls have about their fathers is that they don't feel respected. During adolescence, girls are extremely sensitive to their fathers' feelings about them and may assume they know their fathers' feelings, even when they do not. When (or if) a father seems to be having trouble adjusting to his daughter's new and more mature identity, she probably interprets this state as rejection. Just as with her mother, a girl wants to feel valued by her father for being herself—the self she is becoming.[3]

The process of "letting go" must be carefully and sensitively controlled and monitored. Encouraging your daughter to take responsibility by making choices will entail a process of weaning her from your (and her mother's) authority to allow her the freedom to fail. This weaning process must be:

- intentional
- communicated
- negotiated

Try the following exercise with your daughter:

## Daughter Autonomy Inventory

To fathers:
For each of the following areas, circle the number you think best represents your daughter's ability to be in control of her decisions. Then guess where she thinks her ability is.

1 = she's not ready yet    7 = no problem, she's in charge.

| Choices | Father's view | Daughter's view |
|---|---|---|
| Watching television | 1 2 3 4 5 6 7 | 1 2 3 4 5 6 7 |
| Choosing movies to view | 1 2 3 4 5 6 7 | 1 2 3 4 5 6 7 |
| Choosing friends to talk to | 1 2 3 4 5 6 7 | 1 2 3 4 5 6 7 |

| | | |
|---|---|---|
| Choosing friends to hang out with | 1 2 3 4 5 6 7 | 1 2 3 4 5 6 7 |
| Choosing friends to spend a<br>  weekend with | 1 2 3 4 5 6 7 | 1 2 3 4 5 6 7 |
| Having a curfew | 1 2 3 4 5 6 7 | 1 2 3 4 5 6 7 |
| Doing homework | 1 2 3 4 5 6 7 | 1 2 3 4 5 6 7 |
| Choosing activities and involvements | 1 2 3 4 5 6 7 | 1 2 3 4 5 6 7 |
| Picking college or a post-high school<br>  option | 1 2 3 4 5 6 7 | 1 2 3 4 5 6 7 |
| Finding and getting a job | 1 2 3 4 5 6 7 | 1 2 3 4 5 6 7 |
| Involvement at church (or other<br>  Christian activities) | 1 2 3 4 5 6 7 | 1 2 3 4 5 6 7 |
| Dating (choosing guys to date, choosing<br>  whether to date, et cetera) | 1 2 3 4 5 6 7 | 1 2 3 4 5 6 7 |
| Choice of music | 1 2 3 4 5 6 7 | 1 2 3 4 5 6 7 |

To daughters:

For each of the following areas, circle the number you think best represents your ability to be in control of your decisions. Try to guess where your father would place your ability.

1 = I'm not ready yet    7 = no problem, I'm in charge.

| Choices | Father's view | Daughter's view |
|---|---|---|
| Watching television | 1 2 3 4 5 6 7 | 1 2 3 4 5 6 7 |
| Choosing movies to view | 1 2 3 4 5 6 7 | 1 2 3 4 5 6 7 |
| Choosing friends to talk to | 1 2 3 4 5 6 7 | 1 2 3 4 5 6 7 |
| Choosing friends to hang out with | 1 2 3 4 5 6 7 | 1 2 3 4 5 6 7 |
| Choosing friends to spend a<br>  weekend with | 1 2 3 4 5 6 7 | 1 2 3 4 5 6 7 |
| Having a curfew | 1 2 3 4 5 6 7 | 1 2 3 4 5 6 7 |
| Doing homework | 1 2 3 4 5 6 7 | 1 2 3 4 5 6 7 |
| Choosing activities and involvements | 1 2 3 4 5 6 7 | 1 2 3 4 5 6 7 |

| | | |
|---|---|---|
| Picking college or a post-high school option | 1 2 3 4 5 6 7 | 1 2 3 4 5 6 7 |
| Finding and getting a job | 1 2 3 4 5 6 7 | 1 2 3 4 5 6 7 |
| Involvement at church (or other Christian activities) | 1 2 3 4 5 6 7 | 1 2 3 4 5 6 7 |
| Dating (choosing guys to date, choosing whether to date, et cetera) | 1 2 3 4 5 6 7 | 1 2 3 4 5 6 7 |
| Choice of music | 1 2 3 4 5 6 7 | 1 2 3 4 5 6 7 |

After both of you have completed this exercise, share your results with each other. Be prepared for your daughter to disagree with you, Dad. She may not, and you will know you're doing fine in this area. But for most father-daughter relationships, autonomy is not an easy issue. This exercise will at least get you talking! Now the door is open for future discussion and negotiation.

### A Warm Embrace

A recent study found that adolescents have strong feelings when it comes to their fathers. One question, "What are your top suggestions for improving communication between fathers and adolescents?" garnered many suggestions. Here are the top nine responses.

1. Share feelings, not just thoughts
2. Learn to listen more than talk
3. Don't jump to conclusions
4. Learn to have an open mind
5. Tell the truth, no matter what
6. Be flexible
7. Control anger
8. Invest in me—spend time with me
9. Don't be critical[4]

Adolescents want their fathers to be real and to care about them.

Another factor that emerged from the same study showed that teenagers who perceived their fathers to be "emotionally available" scored nearly twice as high on the "Spiritual Wellness Inventory" (an instrument used to measure spiritual maturity, growth, and interest) than those who perceived their fathers to be "emotionally unavailable" (defined as "simply not close to their fathers").[5]

The authors infer from these two sets of data that there seems to be a connection between how close daughters feel to their fathers and the depth of their faith. While many factors undoubtedly contribute to such a nebulous notion as "spiritual wellness," the results of this study are significant enough to note.

The study did not show conclusively which factor was more responsible for the relationship between fathers and daughters—whether a daughter who takes her Christian faith seriously is more committed to a close relationship with her father or a daughter who has a father who has cultivated a close friendship with her enhances spiritual maturity and growth. Somehow, the relationship between a daughter's perception of father-closeness and her possession of a rich, deep faith is very strong. Therefore, it's safe to conclude that a father who is caring and connected to his daughter will likely see the fruit of that relationship in her own faith.

Your daughter wants you to be involved in her life. She wants to know that you care about her as a unique individual and that you ultimately trust her. Her ability to learn how to make wise choices, as well as how she will see herself in the future, is intimately connected with how close she feels to you.

What does she really want? A warm embrace. A hug. A flower. A card. A serious talk. A few questions. She wants her dad to treat her like a capable, smart, and gifted young woman who, although she will make mistakes along the way, knows that her dad is her greatest fan!

As you cheer your daughter on through her adolescent years, you will be handing her a great incentive to make the kind of choices that honor her, you, and God as she strives to develop personal autonomy.

# CHAPTER EIGHT

# A Father's Love as a Model of the Father's Love

Dear Screw Up (Father),

I'd just like to say, thanks for being there for me when I needed a dad! Because of you I have never had a real father figure in my life since you left. Do you know how hard it has been for my little brother? He has had to grow up with three girls. How would you feel? My little sister doesn't trust any adult males anymore because of you.

—Mary, 15, San Antonio, TX

In March 1997, an episode of the television series "Chicago Hope" was dedicated entirely to the father-son relationship. The show ended with the two main character doctors sitting in a lounge area. One casually remarked to the other: "Why is it that we spend our lives trying to earn our parents' approval?"

The other doctor replied, just as casually, "And do you think they know it?" No answer.

Then the first asked, "Will we ever stop needing each other's approval?"

## From Dee
### Memories of An Adult Daughter

Young women respond in one of two ways concerning their faith as it relates to their relationship with their fathers. Some allow their own sense of a father's rejection to provide a reason not to trust the heavenly Father. For others, a sense of disconnectedness can actually drive them into a deep and rich faith experience. For these girls, however, the road to faith is often a long and painful journey. My life reflected this path.

Instead of transferring my fear of abandonment and loneliness to God, deep inside I was painfully aware of my need for the unconditional love God offered me in Christ Jesus. This awareness came about as a result of many painful years of independent, futile searching for my earthly father's love. The father-love I longed for was a love God the Father had designed to reflect His perfect love and to serve as a bridge to help me know Him. Unfortunately, my solo trek led me down paths of

*(continued)*

"I guess we'll just have to wait and see." The camera then panned back, and the shot slowly faded to black.

The truth of this interchange is a sober reminder to every parent. We have such power over our children. How we influence them can last their lifetime.

We've received far more letters from teenage girls expressing disappointment toward fathers and their failures than we did encouraging or positive ones. Many were addressed to fathers who had left home or perhaps still lived at home but were functionally absent. The pain in these girls runs deep.

By now, we hope we've made it clear that a loving father has a huge impact on the self-esteem and personal confidence of his adolescent daughter. The reverse situation, however, is true as well. An absent father, simply by default, often creates a deep insecurity in his daughter. She may have a hard time feeling worthy of love. Or she may feel unable to find any man—or any adult for that matter—who cares for her as a person. Daughters in this situation will often look for deep and intimate relationships with boys in order to fill the painful hole left by an inaccessible father. And a stern, distant, or abusive father has the potential to set loose even more devastation to his daughter's sense of self for years to come.

Whether you're a highly involved and

loving father or a distant, hard, and disconnected father, one consequence of your relationship with your daughter is sobering, at best: Whatever you have taught her about the notion of "fatherhood," chances are she will carry that into her understanding and practice of faith. While there is little solid research to prove it, there seems to be for most women a connection between how she views her father and how she feels and thinks about the heavenly Father. Take the case of Julie, a thirty-five-year-old counselor at a youth conference we spoke at.

Julie's dad was technically present, but when he was home he was distant at best and mildly abusive at worst. Julie didn't recall any serious beatings. But a tenseness existed around the house when her father was home, especially when he was drinking. I had delivered a message about God being our "biggest fan," using Romans 8:31 as a text: "If God is for us, who can be against us?" Julie approached me, knowing that we were writing this book on father-daughter relationships. She began bluntly: "My dad was no fan!"

She went on to share her story of a stern, distant father who still scares her to this day. The longer we talked, the more bitter she became. She worked hard at convincing me that she had been in therapy and was "clean" with him. But my observation was that she had allowed his claws

exploration with sex, drugs, and alcohol before I realized that the only One who could completely meet the needs of my life was my heavenly Father. To me, a bruised and broken daughter, this concept held incredible power and relief. It took years, but my ultimate response to God's offer of love was a passionate abandonment of my running heart to leap into the arms of protection and strength I had longed for as a child and now experience in my heavenly Father.

Some say parenting in the twentieth century is overrated. I believe that while our children ultimately belong to God, parents—especially fathers—have the responsibility and unique opportunity to flesh out the truth of God's constant, unconditional love. Don't worry, Dads, daughters don't need perfection. What your daughter wants and needs is the honest, open, and loving presence of a father who will help her walk through life. Have courage and step up to the plate of your daughter's world. It's an investment you will never regret.

to dig deeply into her soul. Her father was still a powerful, antagonistic figure in her life, even though Julie described herself as a happily married mother of three.

As I probed more deeply, she made an interesting statement: "I also have a hard time thinking of God as a father. If He's anything like my dad, I don't want anything to do with Him!" With that as a finale, she turned and walked away, saying that she had to go "spend time with her girls." I never saw her again. But her comment disturbed me and still does. Julie had been moved by the message of Romans 8:31, but she was torn apart by the image of a father who is a fan. Her heart had been so bruised by her own father that to imagine God as a loving, passionate, and active father was the ultimate contradiction.

I find it a frightening thought that how a father relates to his kids will affect how they will experience God. When Jesus brought the great and powerful, yet distant, Yahweh home by calling him "our Father," He placed a great deal of pressure on dads. We now carry the same title of the all-loving, all-powerful, and perfect Father in heaven. But once our Lord said it, we as fathers had to come to grips with the implications of such a comparison.

### The Fatherhood of God

Jesus said these words: "And do not call anyone on earth 'father,' for you have one Father, and he is in heaven" (Matthew 23:9). What does it mean that God is our Father?

The first and most obvious issue when discussing the fatherhood of God is the nature of God Himself. Even the use of the male pronoun in that last sentence presents a rhetorical gender emphasis. Many people would not be offended by saying "He" when naming God. In fact, many would probably be more offended if we didn't use a masculine pronoun to refer to God. But in today's culture, some people are offended with the concept of God as solely masculine. The most theological argument is found in the Creation narrative in Genesis 1:27: "So God created man in his own image, in the image of God he created him; male and female he created them." If God *created* gender, then God must be *above* and *beyond* gender.

Although space and the intent of this book prohibit discussing this subject in depth, suffice it to say that theologians generally agree that God is indeed the author of gender. This means that God is not masculine. As noted theologians Bruce Demarest and Gordon Lewis state:

> Distinct from the physical aspects of human personhood, God transcends the physical aspects of both maleness and femaleness. However, since God created both male and female in his image, we may think of both as like God in their distinctively nonphysical, personal male and female qualities. Both male and female are personal in the likeness of God who is personal. From this perspective, scriptural uses of masculine personal pronouns for God (and other male designations such as "Father") primarily convey the connotation of God's personal qualities.[1]

This represents the mainstream of theological thought that God's apparent maleness is actually a way to describe God's personhood linguistically. Referring to God as Father is not to say that He is male but that His fatherhood is an invitation to intimate communion with Him as His children. In Henri Nouwen's masterful work, *The Return of the Prodigal Son,* he describes the heart of this Father in relation to His children:

> As Father, the only authority he claims for himself is the authority of compassion. That authority comes from letting the sins of his children pierce his heart. There is no lust, greed, anger, resentment, jealousy, or vengeance in

his lost children that has not caused immense grief to his heart. The grief is so deep because the heart is so pure. From the deep inner place where love embraces all human grief, the Father reaches out to his children. The touch of his hands, radiating inner light, seeks only to heal. . . .

Here is the God I want to believe in: a Father who, from the beginning of creation, has stretched out his arms in merciful blessing, never forcing himself on anyone, but always waiting.[2]

This is the same Father who spoke to Moses, grieved over Israel's rebellion, and sent His Son into the world as a baby. This is the Father to whom Jesus introduced us and called us to know, love, and serve. God our Father is our merciful, gentle, respectful, powerful, and patient Parent/King. As Paul wrote to the Corinthians, "for us there is but one God, the Father, from whom all things came and for whom we live; and there is but one Lord, Jesus Christ, through whom all things came and through whom we live" (1 Corinthians 8:6).

This same Father is the model and ultimate standard for every father. Again, Paul reminds us of this: "For this reason I kneel before the Father, from whom his whole family in heaven and on earth derives its name" (Ephesians 3:14-15). Our role as fathers, then, and the very structure of the family, are but pictures of true family as revealed in Christ Jesus and His relationship with the Father.

### A Father Who Draws His Daughter to God

Recent studies have shown that the number-one predictor of children who go on in their faith is the lived-out faith of their parents. It is not the nature of the church community nor the denomination, and it is not even the quality of a church youth ministry, although those programs are a tremendous support to parents. What makes committed young disciples is parents who consistently live out their faith both in words and in lifestyle.

If you have read this far, you know about the power and impact you have with your daughter as she is growing up. You know that her understanding of who God is, how He feels about her, and even how He has called her to live has a great deal to do with you. How you love your daughter and treat her will do far more for her future faith than years of "family devotions" and keeping religious rules and expectations. It may sound contradictory, but fathers who have strictly enforced "spiritual" rules and have structured the family around "religious" activities can sometimes cause the exact opposite response that they desire in their children.

> Dear Dad,
> Thanks for everything you have done for me. I really appreciate it. But there is one thing. Why do we have to do family devotions? It's boring! Everybody hates it, even you, it seems like, but we still have to do it.
>
> —Crystal, 13, Ft. Walton Beach, FL

It's true that faith is meant to be passed on to our kids. God is very clear about this:

> These commandments that I give you today are to be upon your hearts. Impress them on your children. Talk about them when you sit at home and when you walk along the road, when you lie down and when you get up. (Deuteronomy 6:6-7)

How we "impress them" on our children is the key. If we are loving and gentle with our daughters, and our faith penetrates deeper than mere activity and devotional duty, we communicate by our lives that God is real and He matters to us. This is what our children need to see.

Fathers who want more than anything else to draw their daughters to their heavenly Father would do well to heed these four characteristics of a godly father. He

- loves his wife
- lives and then dispenses mercy and justice
- fights against the seduction of power
- seeks to live an authentic life

### Love Your Wife

In 1997, two professors from Abilene Christian University completed a ten-year study of church-raised adolescents' attitudes and perceptions of their fathers.[3] In the article titled, "How Do Fathers Help Turn Their Teenagers' Hearts Toward Christ?" the top issue mentioned was, "By setting an example for the family ('walk the walk')."

Today's young people, as Generation-X literature overwhelmingly affirms, are incredibly astute in their ability to judge the hearts and motives of people. For adolescent girls this is even more true. Their relational antennae are always active. If your daughter senses that her mother is not being cared for or treated with kindness, compassion, and respect by you, it's doubtful that you will be able to influence her positively for God's kingdom. If, on the other hand, she can feel that her mother is married to a man who honors and empowers her, your daughter will be far more open to allowing your faith to penetrate her life.

When you love your wife, you are loving each of your kids. You are also modeling the faith you profess.

### Dispense Justice and Mercy

Both justice and mercy are aspects of the heavenly Father's character. God, in His justice, is good, right, honest, pure, and holy. Our God is passionate in His wrath against sin and His zeal for righteousness. In addition, God, in His mercy, is gentle, forgiving, and compassionate toward those who fail and fall down. Our God is equally passionate about His mercy, grace, and kindness. God is both holy and caring, righteous and forgiving, just and the One who justifies.

We, on the other hand, have difficulty balancing these characteristics. The father who tends toward kindness often has a hard time dispensing judgment and discipline when confronted with an offense. The father who esteems holiness may be less than merciful when his child fails. Both extremes are detrimental to a daughter's growth as a believer. She will be far better off with a father who seeks to balance justice and mercy and who lives them as a package instead of two polar opposites.

The high road of modeling God's character is difficult, but every father must train and discipline himself to humbly seek a balance between lofty moralizing and sentimental acquiescence. To model God's love, a father must clearly be committed to a life of truth, integrity, and purity. But he must also remember his own up-and-down spiritual journey. Yes, teach your daughter to seek goodness, to value righteousness, and to abhor sin as well as oppression. As you work hard to help train up your daughter in these things, recognize that God takes a lifetime with you—with all of us, patiently guiding and nudging us to the next level of lived-out righteousness. Therefore, you must discipline your daughter appropriately when she needs correction and carefully instruct and correct her without humiliating, defeating, or being relationally invasive toward her. As Paul writes, "Fathers, do not exasperate your children; instead, bring them up in the training and instruction of the Lord" (Ephesians 6:4).

### Fight Against the Seduction of Power
Power is perhaps the greatest enemy of the truth. It lies to us: "You will truly *be somebody!*" It deceives: "You know better than

they do." It divides: "I am to be obeyed!"

Power rears its head in a variety of ways that can impact the father-daughter relationship. First, the need for power can cause a father to spend far more energy and effort in the workplace and in work-related relationships than with his family. Work's allure is easily rationalized: "This position (or person) will help my career, and that will be better for my family." But your daughter is far more concerned with knowing you as a person and watching how you view life.

In the workplace we feel that if we're going to carve out a niche that will impact our family, it's up to us. That's true, to a point. But when the drive to succeed at work spills over into a need for more power, prestige, or an evergrowing niche, or we allow ourselves to lose sight of what *really* is important, this striving is misplaced. It is up to God to build power and influence in our careers as we are faithful, kind, and diligent — but not obsessive — in our work.

Second, how a father wields power in the family sends a signal to an adolescent daughter about her father's desire to connect intimately with and love the other members of the family. If you are a father who needs to be in control, if you want the family to revolve around your life, your interests, and your schedule, then other family members — especially your daughter — may come to resent you. Yes, a father (along with his wife) must exert some form of leadership in the family. But godly leadership is more an exercise in empowering other family members than an inner drive to control them.

Third, how a father sees his power in the church will model for his family what it means to participate in the local family of God. How does your daughter see or experience your dissatisfaction, frustration, or anguish over the issues in your church? Do you present an attitude that is marked by humility, prayer, and healthy relationships? Or are you one who "makes known your position" and "speaks your mind"?

In our experience in the church and other Christian organizations, we've seen many people use power to control, divide, or even destroy ministries and relationships. Often, the children of these people are the losers, for they learn how to participate in churches and Christian institutions by throwing their weight around and vying to get their own way.

Teach your daughter not to seek power for power's sake. And when she is given power and influence, demonstrate how she can use it for God's glory and not her own.

## Seek to Live an Authentic Life

Compartmentalization is perhaps the greatest single issue facing men of faith today. Modern men have perfected the art of pretense. On the inside they may feel fear and loneliness, but they learn at a young age to mask that fear behind a wall of superiority, busyness, and effective perseverance. They neatly package and shelve the things that bother them, hurt them, or cause them to feel insecure. *I'll deal with it later,* a man may think. But on the shelf these things fester, ooze, and drip, penetrating the soul like slowly burning embers. Still, our intrinsic bent is to ignore our pain. Fueled by the fear of being discovered, we move in and out of relationships, always subtly conscious that we are vulnerable to anyone who can see inside us.

Men involved in the church are not immune from this cultural malaise. In fact, they may suffer from it even more than others do. For many Christian men, the church is the most threatening place to be. They can easily feel that church is where they have to pretend the most. However, Christianity has only the power to heal those who can admit their brokenness, for Jesus Christ is Lord only when pretense is set aside.

It should be obvious by now that your daughter can tell what is real and what isn't. You can't hide from such a relationally intuitive machine as an adolescent girl who cares for you. How we fathers deal with our inner lives reveals the core honesty of our faith. Your daughter knows you well, and she loves you anyway. She can tell if you play at faith or if you really mean it. She can see if your prayers, your involvement in Christian activities, and your convictions flow from a soul that has been taken captive by the overwhelming grace of God. As author and speaker Brennan Manning has said, she will take notice if your heart has been "seized by the power of a great affection."

To live an authentic life means that you strive to live as one set free. Fear and failure can be your most strident adversaries when you empower them by concealment and denial. To live out authentic faith, you must consistently dredge the depths of your heart, experiences, values, and relationships. You must willingly present whatever you find to the God who quietly waits with healing compassion and fierce mercy.

For your daughter's faith to be set free, she needs to see *your* faith set free. Although never a father, St. Francis of Assisi knew what it meant to pass on the faith to our adolescent children. He said: "Preach Christ at all times—if necessary, use words!"

*Dear Dad,*

*There are a great many things I could tell you but have never had the strength since I know we'd both be moved to tears so fast that nothing would come out right. My Father in heaven has so richly blessed me with the perfect father on earth. Without knowing it, you have shaped so much of my personality and built so much of my faith. I want you to know how much I truly love and appreciate you and every sacrifice, little and big, you have made for me throughout my life. Most of all, I am grateful for the loving, Christ-centered household in which you chose to raise a family. So much of your laughter and love lives within me. Thank you for the beautiful example you have* set for my future household and family. Thank you for putting up with me and loving me unconditionally. Thank you for being my friend. You are an amazing man of God, Dad.

I love you with all of my heart!

—Teri, 21, Austin, TX

# CHAPTER NINE

# Being Her Teacher When You Want to Be Her Judge

*Dad,*
*You've been an excellent dad, as much as you could. But when I was a young child, you didn't seem to have enough time for me. Now that I'm older, I don't have the time for you. Now you need me. It's hard to build a father-daughter relationship when I barely see you, and when I do you act more like a strict priest than my father.*

—Linda, 16, St. Louis, MO

Mr. Johnson was the best teacher our kids ever had. He was warm and friendly—the prototypical Teddy Bear. When a student went to talk to him, this fifth grade teacher stopped what he was doing, sat down on the edge of a desk to get on eye level with the budding adolescent, and listened with care and interest. When he got mad (as our kids tell it), he got mad! But just as quickly, he would turn around, smile, and offer a word of encouragement. He was a tough but fair grader. He would never overlook anyone, and he wouldn't allow himself to believe negative or harsh words that previous teachers had written

## From Dee
### Memories of an Adult Daughter

—

No daughter wants a judge as a father. Some don't even want a teacher! What a young woman does want in her dad is someone she can trust and believe in. To a daughter, her father is often like a judge who is distant, clear-cut, and lives by the book. I remember my dad acting this way, but by the time I was fifteen, I nodded and then did what I wanted to do. The judge "thing" didn't work for me, and I doubt that it works for many girls. A daughter just doesn't want to be parented by a distant judge.

A father who is a teacher will be welcomed if he's a good teacher. A good teacher listens first, *then* responds. A good teacher is able to laugh with his students and cares more about the final knowledge gained than about grades or tests. Every girl needs a father who is committed to being a good teacher.

My father was not a teacher, good *or* bad. He was

*(continued)*

about one of his students. He was determined to bring out the best in every precious boy or girl he taught.

Miss Claypool was not the best teacher our kids ever had. She was all business, which is not necessarily bad. But she had a style that communicated a coldness you could almost feel when she entered the classroom. There was a poster on her wall that read, "Do it right the first time," and another, "School rules will be strictly enforced." Her students were orderly and well mannered. But there were few smiles, and some of the slower kids kept falling further and further behind those who were temperamentally suited to her way of doing things. Homework was handed in on time or it was not accepted. She was fair, consistent, and ruled with a heavy hand.

Mr. Johnson's kids were wild, fun, happy, and growing like weeds in every way. His class scores and marks improved in record numbers each year—across the board. Miss Claypool's kids were stiff and controlled. The best students, academically speaking, improved; the ones who struggled, regressed. Mr. Johnson was a teacher of individual kids on a journey. Miss Claypool was a controlling judge who maintained appropriate order. Every one of Mr. Johnson's students felt loved, supported, and encouraged. Miss Claypool's class felt structured, driven, and stereotyped. Each of the kids in Mr. Johnson's class went on to excel in middle school, but many of Miss Claypool's continued to scramble just to survive.

What makes a good teacher for someone who needs to grow but whose life seems to be in a constant state of turmoil? Does it take order, structure, and control? Or does it take a committed, concerned, and available fan?

a judge. I didn't want a judge, and I wouldn't listen to a judge. Now I know that I longed for a kind, gentle, smart, forward-thinking teacher!

A father who wants to give his daughter the best shot at a full life must resist the temptation to be a strict and rational controller or even a kind and benevolent judge. For her to realize fully what it means to live as an adult who knows and likes herself, and is responsible for her choices, dad must shift roles and become a gentle and focused teacher. A judging father tells his daughter right from wrong, instructs her on the way to live, and authoritatively dispenses rulings and directives. At this stage of her life, she is far more in need of a dad who teaches her how to distinguish for herself what is right and what is wrong.

In light of the concepts we have presented, look at the differences between a father-judge and a father-teacher:

| Needs | Judge | Teacher |
|---|---|---|
| Identity | "Here's who I want you to be." | "Let's discover who you are." |
| Autonomy | "Here's what I want you to do." | "What do *you* want to do?" "How can I help you?" |
| Trust | "You trust me." | "I trust you." |
| Communication | "*I* will talk to you, and you speak when you are spoken to." | "I will listen to *you* and I will share with *you* my heart." |
| Closeness | "You are a part of this family; act accordingly." | "I love you and I believe in you." "I want you to know I'll always be there for you." |

You have a choice every time you bump up against your adolescent daughter's needs in the areas of identity, autonomy, trust, communication, or closeness. You can either be a father-judge or a father-teacher. Let's look at what this means for each need.

### *Identity*

When a convicted criminal faces a judge, he is at the directive mercy of that judge. It's not the *person* who wears the robe that matters. The criminal and the judge may be neighbors. They may volunteer in the same organization or even attend the same church. But an inherent authority and a certain style accompanies the role of judge.

In terms of a daughter's sense of identity, a father may love his little girl so much that he falls into playing the role of judge in her life. He may sense who she is, or what he perceives she ought to be, based on his love for her. He may even be correct in his assessment. But every time a father dictates to his daughter who she is, or even who she ought to be, he drives a stake right through the heart of their relationship. He also hinders her ability to discover who she is for herself.

On the other hand, a father who strives to teach, though he may care no more deeply than the judge, is aware and careful with his words and manner because he knows that his daughter's greatest need is to discover for herself who she is. The teacher-father is a helping, gentle instructor who listens to his daughter and gently pushes her to consider the best for her life.

This sounds so simple to do, but years of history as well as emotional and relational patterns are hard to discard. When a daughter hits adolescence, a father simply has to remember to leave the judge's robe in the closet. He must gently teach his daughter how to think about herself without controlling and dominating the process in an attempt to force her to see his view of her.

A father-teacher who wants to help his daughter in her quest for identity must keep the teacher's task foremost in mind. That task is to *instruct the student but not do the work of the student*. It is crucial that dads make this shift with daughters who are approaching adolescence.

When your daughter was young, you (and her mother) thought through all the options in a given situation or circumstance and told your child how she was to act or what she was to do. Now that she's an adolescent, the father-teacher's role is to listen to her, then gently but clearly remind her that she is still "in the classroom" and needs your input. It is equally important to communicate that the outcome of her thinking ultimately rests with her.

This change must take place incrementally over time. In terms of her identity, a father's goal is to help a daughter see herself in light of her relationship with God by focusing on His love demonstrated for her in creation and redemption. God made her unique. He loved her enough and found her precious enough to send His Son to die and rise again for her. The father-teacher's task is to continually bring his daughter back to this truth. He must strive, as respectfully and gently as possible, to help her see that all she is can only be discovered through the love and calling of Jesus Christ.

### Autonomy

As a teacher, a father carries the responsibility to provide information for his daughter to act on. When it comes to autonomy, he has the advantage of having seen, over the course of a lifetime, the power of consequence. This depth of experience is a tremendous gift a father can give his daughter as she goes through adolescence, yet it must be handled with great care and savvy. When asked for input on a specific decision, for example, a father-judge may say to his daughter, "You can't do that! You should do this! When I was a kid. . . ."

In comparison, a father-teacher would probably respond with something like, "Think of a few different things that could happen with each of your options. Together, let's look at three possible consequences of each decision."

A father-teacher knows that unless his daughter learns how to make decisions, and understands and *even suffers the appropriate consequences herself,* she will not grow into healthy womanhood. She will constantly be looking for others to decide for her. That is far worse than most anything she will do under her father's loving tutelage.

It is vital to remember that the journey into adolescence is very difficult on a daughter, but especially in the area of autonomy. As Patricia H. Davis points out:

> Although gender roles are slowly changing, men's traditional 'natural' realm is the public; men have been expected to introduce girls to what it means to have competence and mastery outside of the home.

For this reason, a father's expectations of his daughter hold extreme importance for her. In the best cases, a father's support becomes the validation a daughter needs to confirm her own independent identity. A father who promotes his daughter's drive for achievement is telling her that a powerful part of her emerging identity is valued by those she loves. It is often difficult, however, in this androcentric culture, for fathers to figure out what it is they expect from (or for) their daughters.[1]

Your daughter is walking a tightrope between two worlds—one where she must completely rely on you (and your authority in her life) and another where she is completely responsible for herself. Imagine a daughter who has been told what to do, how to think, and how to act throughout her high school years. She graduates and leaves home for the large college two hundred miles away. In the first week she is accosted with invitations to drink and do drugs; she meets dozens of twentysomething young "dudes" with hyperactive hormones, who want to "spend the weekend" with her; and she has a roommate who has been a self-described "hard-core party-er" since age twelve. How do you think the daughter would fare in this environment?

Think of your own daughter. Is she prepared for the real world?

> *Dear Dad,*
> *I'm not who you think I am. You still see me in my Sunday school dress and a cute ribbon in my hair. But you have no idea what it is like at school. Everybody drinks and has sex, and I am like everybody else. I don't want to hurt you, but you never let me out of your "cage" growing up. I didn't know what to expect. Well, I do now, and I'm sorry. I feel bad even admitting these things, but you had to know.*
> —Name and age withheld, youth worker conference in Anaheim, CA

As your daughter attempts to control her own life and make decisions, she needs you to teach her how and to encourage her in the process. For her own good, you really have no choice but to do this! A healthy, loving family becomes the adolescent's "life-laboratory" in which she has the relative freedom to test out her own way of making decisions and discovering for herself a value system she can use to guide her. This is difficult and may feel very risky, but the consequences in this type of an environment are generally not nearly so severe as they would be if she waited until she was on her own.

We're not saying that anything goes, and we're not advocating that you throw open the doors to her lifestyle and choices. Be a teacher, and treat her accordingly (even Mr. Johnson yelled and disciplined the students when they didn't behave responsibly). But teach her nonetheless.

A father-teacher will have a hard time watching his little girl flail and stumble, but he will be way ahead in the parenting game if he's there to pick her up and dust her off. As long as you are present and involved, like any good teacher, at least she has a chance.

### Trust

The father-judge, even as his daughter grows older, remains primarily concerned that his daughter trusts him. This is just another way to get her to say, "You know better than me, Dad. I will always listen to you."

In contrast, the father-teacher is committed to moving beyond an authority-down style of parenting so that his daughter knows that, no matter what she does or becomes, he will always believe in her.

This is so hard for many fathers. For most men, trust is wrapped up in performance. We may feel like it's parental suicide to tell our sixteen-year-old that we trust her. If you still feel like that, after reading this far, we urge you to go back and reread chapter three.

Lifestyle, choices, consequences, even discipline are not intrinsic to the notion of trust. Trust is saying to your daughter that, no matter what, you know she will ultimately be the kind of person who knows who she is, makes wise choices, and takes control of her life.

A father-teacher, after his daughter makes a series of poor choices (or even when she is in the throes of rebellion), may say, "You will not be with friends for two weeks, and you've lost the car for a month. But I want you to know that I will walk through this with you as you try to learn from what happened."

Many Christian parenting experts would probably disagree with what we've just said. But we're *not* advocating an abandonment of parental concern or of an appropriate control of authority. *To do so would deny that your daughter still needs you to be her teacher when she is not yet an adult on her own!* But we also firmly believe that for a daughter's growth and future development, she must feel that her parents, and especially her father, truly believe in her, and trust her at the core, even when she fails or makes poor — even destructive — decisions. A father-teacher is not so concerned with the scores on the quizzes, or even the tests, in his classroom; he's in it for the lifetime score his daughter achieves.

Parenting is not for the fainthearted or for those who need to be in charge. (Of course, if you fall into this group, it's too late!) A parent's job is to wean his daughter off dependency on him and enable her to stand tall as an individual.

### Communication

By now you know what your daughter needs from you as a father-teacher. But for most fathers, communication proves to be the biggest downfall. Research consistently affirms that fathers most often disappoint their daughters and sometimes even cause significant damage in this area.[2] Few dads are out to hurt their daughters. But many of us just don't know how to communicate with our daughters in a way that is meaningful for them. At the very least, we are simply uncomfortable when talking with them. Perhaps the problem is in our approach to the communication process.

A judge-communicator controls the communication. He dictates when and where the conversation will take place, the topic(s) to be covered, and the length of time set aside for the talk. "Speak when you are spoken to" is one of the most interpersonally destructive parenting statements ever uttered. A judge uses his gavel to get attention. A judge says, "I will talk, *you* will listen." *Ouch!* In writing this we can now feel ourselves righteously pounding that sacred hammer.

A loving, committed teacher-communicator gets on an eye

level, and a heart level, with his daughter. He watches for the nonverbal cues that map out the relational terrain. He gladly stops whatever he's doing when she raises a hand. He can tell when his instructions are confusing, or if he's gone too fast or too far, or when he's allowed a breach in the relationship by something said (or something not).

A father who seeks to be a teacher will do far more listening than talking. He will also never fail to answer the question "Why?" when misunderstood or even challenged, though it's up to him to ensure that the conversation stays on track and doesn't get too disjointed or emotionally out of hand.

He will give his daughter the benefit of his years of life—his experiences of pain and joy, failure and success, fear and victory—even before she asks. But he will also be keenly aware of timing, moods, and underlying issues that, although not mentioned, may be driving the conversation. In short, a teacher-communicator father will strive to maintain open lines of thought and intimacy through regular and sensitive communication whenever the opportunity presents itself.

### Closeness

The judge's concern is with rules and directives. A judge, by role, cannot afford to get close because intimacy will cause a judge to rule with partiality. Yet a teacher is a better teacher when he or she cares. The teacher's main task is not evaluation, it is development and growth. He or she is concerned with care, instruction, and encouragement.

A father who tries to hold on to his role as the relatively distant and controlling father cannot hope to be close to his daughter. However, closeness is what she needs more than anything.

*Dear Daddy,*
*You used to hug me, and now all you do is yell.*
—Kim, 13, Montgomery, AL

Take off the robe, Dad. She's growing up, and she needs her father to love her, listen to her, and carefully — gently — instruct her in how she is to live.

# CHAPTER TEN

# Being Her Guide When You Want to Be Her Boss

Dear Dad,

This is hard to say (and I probably won't be able to even tell you), but I hate how you try to boss me around all the time. I know you love me, and you tell me that all the time, but I have a hard time feeling like you even know what love means. If you loved me, you would let me grow up. I'm fifteen now, and you treat me like I'm a little kid. I don't need a boss. I need someone to let me make my own decisions.

Remember when we went to the family camp last summer and we took that hike in the mountains? Remember Jeremy our guide? We all needed him and listened to him, but he made it fun for us. He didn't try and tell us where to go, he helped us pick our own trail. Remember how much we all liked that? Daddy, I need a guide more than I need a boss. I love you, but I'm sick of you being my boss. Can't you be my guide? Can't you at least try?

—Sharon, 15, Littleton, CO

*From Dee*
**Memories of an Adult Daughter**

I worked from the time I was fifteen until I got married. I've had some great bosses and a few others I would not wish on anyone. But as much as I liked the good bosses, no father, especially a father of a teenage daughter, will be effective as a boss.

My dad sometimes tried to be my boss. Whenever he did, I would chafe, argue, and fight. He wasn't very good at it (he'd made too many mistakes in our family), but he still thought that because he was the "father" he had the right to tell me (and the rest of his children) what to do. This only drove me further away from him. As long as he refused to get close, and to care about my life, I was determined not to allow him to control my life, *even when he thought he was!*

I have also been under the leadership of a guide. I remember sailing in British Columbia with a group of high school students. Our

*(continued)*

It's a hot day, almost sweltering. As you rush in from a bus that ran five minutes late, you can feel the eyes of the other employees, sharing your fear. You punch the time clock and clumsily rush to your station, hoping your tardiness will go unnoticed. Just as you sit and prepare your spool of coarse wool for the day's quota, you sense his approach. You aren't scared, really, but with a distinct sense of foreboding you glance up to face the duty manager. His eyes tell all. You are being "put on notice," and this is your last warning.

During the boss's speech you feel yourself wanting to run, to hide, or perhaps even fight back, regardless of the consequences. But as you sit and listen, you know you will just sit there, disengaged from the barrage of frustration and anger, waiting for it to end so you can get back to work. No sooner does he turn his back with a shake of his head than you find yourself whispering to a coworker, "I can't wait to get out of this place!"

Consider a second scenario: As the sun rises above the majestic peak of an ancient precipice, you can feel the anticipation of a new day in the wilderness. The crispness of the air, your still-visible breath, the song of a solitary bird having breakfast in a pine tree. "What does the day hold?" you ask. Your guide, a slim, bearded, wolf-like lover of the wild approaches with a warm smile and a warmer cup of coffee. "Where do you want to go today?" he says in reply.

You gaze at the distant peak but hesitate to form the words. "I don't know, really. But, well, that peak looks like fun. But I suppose it's too high, too far, and too difficult for a day's hike."

"Well," he says in a sober tone, "it is a tough climb. There's no easy route. It would take some risk and hard work to make it to the top." Then he is silent. He seems to be waiting for a response.

"I'd like to try, if we could."

A smile. "Okay, then, here are three options we need to discuss, and together we'll look for the best route."

Two types of leaders, as different in style as in function. A *boss* provides both the rules of the road and the instructions on how to get there. Guidelines, objectives, and discipline are the order of the day. A *guide* is a servant, available to offer advice for the journey and help in time of need. With a guide you can count on sincere questions, an attentive ear, and cautious yet gentle encouragement.

Which kind of father does an adolescent daughter need, a boss or a guide? Look at some of the differences between the two:

| **Boss** | **Guide** |
| --- | --- |
| Controller | Advisor |
| Orders | Suggests |
| Talks | Listens |
| An authority | A friend |

"captain" functioned more as a guide than a boss. He never took over, but he was ready to lend a hand or give some suggestions when we needed him (whether we knew it or not!). When it was stormy he stood by the helm, but he never panicked (even when we heeled over so far we thought we were going to capsize). When it was calm he would sit with us and talk about sailing, his love for the water, and he would instill in us the confidence we needed to carry on. I always wanted that kind of dad.

The dad I would have listened to—at least more than I did—was a dad who was willing to stand beside me as I made my way through adolescence, one who would have given me the boundaries I needed to keep from capsizing. I would have listened to a dad who was more interested in helping me navigate life's waters than in controlling my every move. A dad who guides will always be sought out when the wind is blowing. But a boss will not be summoned, even in a storm.

——

When your daughter was little, she needed a boss. She found comfort in a daddy who was in control. She needed and sometimes even wanted clear boundaries and disciplinary enforcement of the rules of the family. Your daughter may have been a compliant, obedient, and even happy little girl. But then, between ages ten and twelve, something began to change. As she entered the beginning stages of adolescence, your daughter instinctively knew that she was entering a phase of life where she was ultimately in charge of her own life. It's not that she sought this change. In fact, she may have tried to stall it. But the move from dependence to interdependence in the family was inevitable.

Perhaps you were not ready for such a change, but something had begun to click inside of her. She could sense that she needed to be more than a cute little girl who simply nodded at her mom and dad's ordering of her life. Her heart was aching at the loss of childhood, yet bursting with the hope of becoming a woman. She knew she had to grow up, and she needed her dad's help.

What kind of help does an adolescent daughter need? She needs the loving leadership of a guide!

The following chart represents the differences between how a guide and a boss might perceive their roles:

| NEEDS | BOSS | GUIDE |
|---|---|---|
| Identity | "Here's the task before you—just do it." | "Who does God want you to become?" |
| Autonomy | "I am your father. The Bible says you must obey me." | "You will soon be an adult; the Bible says not to discourage you." |
| Trust | "I need to know that I can count on you." | "I need you to know that you can count on me." |
| Communication | "Be careful what you say to me." | "I'm always ready to talk about it." |
| Closeness | "Do what's expected of you and we'll always get along fine." | "Please don't cut yourself off; we need each other." |

Let's take a look at how the two types of fathers—the boss and the guide—relate to the five key needs of an adolescent daughter.

### Identity

A father-guide is a question asker; a father-boss is a question answerer. As a daughter walks through the changes that come with adolescence, she is constantly attempting to distinguish between the voices that compete for her attention. Some of these messages try to shove her into a box that may or may not fit her: "Be pretty"; "Be smart"; "Be like everyone else"; "Be different"; "Talk like this"; "Dress like that." Other messages seek to shape her identity in the roles she is expected to play and the things she's able to do: "Be a doctor"; "Go to college"; "Don't waste your athletic skill. You're a great dancer."

The voices may mean well; they may even think they're being loving and encouraging. But as the voices shout out the variety of roles, expectations, and desires your daughter is to fulfill, she will most likely feel overwhelmed instead of knowing who she sees herself to be. Each voice presents a path into the mist. With so many paths to choose from, your daughter may have a hard time deciding which way to go. The fog can get quite thick and foreboding. As the voices cry out, your daughter desperately needs a guide.

In terms of identity, a father-guide will repeat one message in a variety of ways and contexts: "As God's blessed and beloved child, who do you see yourself to be?" Your daughter may tire at being reminded of the same basic identity question, but the repetition serves two purposes: It lets her know that you care about her process of discovering who she is, and it constantly brings her back to seeing herself in light of who God sees her to be. Your job as a father-guide is simple and straightforward. You are to encourage your daughter to live as the one she knows herself to be. In this way, you will help her far more than if you tell her who she is to you.

### Autonomy

It is a rare but smart boss who encourages those under his authority to make decisions and think for themselves. In management circles the tendency to overcontrol employees is called "micromanaging." A smart, well-trained boss will grant enough authority to match the responsibility required for someone under his charge.

Similarly, a good guide will not allow someone to do something dangerous or foolish. He knows how to steer those he is guiding away from danger, while still allowing and even encouraging them to call the shots.

For a father, conveying and commanding the ultimate authority of a boss and expressing the thoughtful and committed concern of a guide requires a delicate balance. When a father slips into the boss category, his daughter will likely sense his desire to control her, and she will pull back. The older she gets, the more important the role of father-guide becomes. Eventually, your daughter will be gone, and the only hold you'll have on her will be as a distant guide. And that's only if she allows you even that much of a role in her life.

Almost every daughter knows that she needs a guide and will, generally speaking, welcome a father who is committed to playing that role as she develops her own sense of autonomy. Most daughters will make decisions that a father-boss could not tolerate as they try out the wings of anticipated freedom. Many of their decisions will even make a father-guide nervous. One young woman wrote on the Internet to a group of youth workers in a youth ministry chat room about this very tendency:

> Teenagers are so confused. We don't know who we are
> or who we want to be. We want to see what else there is

in life. We want to try and dare to do the things that Mom and Dad always say no to.

We're dying for discussions that will bring us together to talk about real issues. We have hurts and worries and things we don't know exactly how to deal with. We want to talk about deeper things. To be honest with you, we want to know more about how God can really relate to us.

I ask one thing. I beg of you. Please do not ignore us, nor what we deal with.[1]

This young woman's letter was to Christian youth workers, and she was speaking to those who lead youth ministries across the country. But her cry must be heard by fathers, for the poignant call for relevant youth ministry is also a wake-up cry for fathers who want to help their daughters during this turbulent season of their lives.

The young woman claims that young people want to talk about deep, real, serious issues. If a father will invest time, energy, and care as his daughter moves through adolescence, she will have less need to find an outside person to be her guide.

It takes years of slowly building trust and weaning her off childlike dependence on you and her mother, but your daughter wants to have someone in her life who will help sort things out as she makes decisions that will affect her future.

### Trust

Both a guide and a boss must have the trust of those they lead, and both need to know that they can trust those they lead. However, there is a difference in emphasis between a boss's view of leadership and a guide's. A guide knows that to be effective, it's more important that his client trust him than for him to trust his client. A boss is more concerned that he can trust his employee.

In the same way, a father-boss will always be questioning whether he can trust his adolescent daughter. But a father-guide focuses on convincing his daughter that he is trustworthy. When he violates that sense of trust, he must do the hardest thing of all on a father's list of duties—ask for forgiveness.

*Dear Dad,*
*Have you ever been wrong? I don't think I have ever heard you say "I'm sorry" without somehow giving an excuse or reason why it wasn't your fault in the first place.*
—Christine, 15, Palo Alto, CA

Why is it so hard for some parents to accept guilt and admit wrongdoing? When we've brought this subject up with kids over the years, most laugh and agree that it's nearly impossible for parents to take responsibility for their behavior.

You may be thinking, "At least here's one area that I have wired. It's not a problem with me." Well, perhaps you're right. But we would like to ask you to try something. Within the next day or two, take a few moments of down time (carve some out if you can't find it) and ask your daughter to respond honestly to the following three questions:

- Do you think I have a hard time admitting when I'm wrong?
- Do you think I am honestly sorry when I've apologized?
- How do you think I could improve in this area?

If your daughter hesitates to answer, even for a moment, then you know *right then* that she's carrying some baggage in this area. If she's afraid to say something, if she hems and haws, or sheepishly says, "No. You're fine," then there is, very likely, a block in her trust in you.

Most parents instinctively feel that they are fully trustworthy, and if their child doesn't trust them, it must be the child's fault. But it's understandable that if your daughter believes you have a hard time owning up to failure and weakness, she will allow that perception to cause a rift in her trust in you.

## Communication

A boss wants his employees to know there are certain things they may and may not say to him. It is somehow tied to a skewed notion of respect for the position. A guide, however, needs information if he is to be a good guide. A boss may need information as well, but in a top-down organization, communication channels and protocol must be respected. A guide is more concerned with the task at hand and the adventure of the journey than he is about channels and modes of communication and appropriate protocol. A guide is in the service business. Therefore, his client needs to be encouraged to speak up and to speak loudly.

The ability to communicate is the greatest gift God has given to His people to build relationships. Communication allows us to have a thought, feeling, or emotion and then pass that same thought, feeling, or emotion on to someone else so they can experience it with us. Communication creates community, warmth, and intimacy. It is the centerpiece of every human activity, endeavor, and relationship.

*Daddy:*

*This letter I've written you is sad because I could never really say these things to your face. I really wish I could be honest, but you are always shutting me off. You are either too tired or too busy or too mad or too whatever! I know it is partly my fault because I don't say things with the proper respect, or I get mad, or you really are tired. But you never want to listen to me, no matter what I do.*

—Kelly, 13, South Bend, IN

Open lines of communication and the modes of communicating are the single most essential tool for the health and depth of the father–adolescent daughter relationship. Any rules, norms, or expectations that block communication will prove destructive to the core of that relationship. It's not just about talking; it's about how you talk, when you talk, and what you talk about that ultimately matters.

A father-guide wants communication wide open when it comes to his daughter. Of course, situations will occur when you need to draw a line in the sand; for instance, when you are overly exhausted or too emotionally charged to connect. But these episodes should be *few and far between and should be the exception, not the rule, to father-daughter communication.* If you recognize that ten o'clock at night is the time when she begins to open up, even though it's your time to go to bed, change your sleep patterns and see these late-night opportunities to talk as holy moments!

If your daughter is most honest when emotionally upset, then as a father-guide you may have to allow her to let off a little steam in order to get at the core of her frustration. Whatever it takes, the goal of the father-guide is to hear what his daughter feels, desires, fears, thinks, and needs. Whenever and however she needs to express that (and this will change over the course of her adolescence), your job is to open the door for her.

### Closeness

A boss may mistakenly believe that he doesn't need his employees. But a guide is well aware that he's intrinsically connected to his client, whether or not the client knows it.

With patience and conviction, a father-guide realizes that he and his daughter are linked for eternity. There will be times when she seems to cut herself off from her dad or seems indifferent to him. A father who has read this book may occasionally get discouraged, sensing that his daughter doesn't like him like other daughters enjoy their dads. Or he may feel that his daughter is somehow different because of a season of time when she doesn't seem to want anything to do with him. But the father-guide knows that this season will pass. He knows it's just his daughter's way of trying to find herself apart from her mother and father.

Sometimes a father can push too hard as he seeks "closeness" out of *his* own needs and from *his* own perspective. But a father-guide must remember that his job is not complete until the very long journey is over. During adolescence, your daughter needs to know that you love her and are committed to her, *regardless* of how she behaves.

If your daughter is wandering away, this may be a sign of a serious problem that needs to be addressed with a qualified Christian elder, friend, or counselor. But it's more likely that distancing herself is just her way of working out something in her life. A father-guide is careful not to push. Rather, he listens and is consistent in his care, concern, and availability.

Dear Daddy,

Growing up in a divorced family was confusing sometimes, but your love for my stepmother was always constant. I was jealous sometimes because I knew you before she knew you. Now, as a young woman, I realize that your love for my stepmother was one of the greatest things you have ever given to me. You taught me how a husband should love his wife. I am very lucky to have a dad like you! I praise God for you.

I love you.

—Erin, 20, San Antonio, TX

# CHAPTER ELEVEN

# Being Her Friend When You Want to Be Her Protector

*Dear Dad,*
*I'm not a baby. Stop calling me that!*

—Steph, 13, Atlanta, GA

More than anything else I want to protect my kids—especially my daughter. I can tell this will be a lifelong struggle for me because, no matter how old she is, I want to keep her from anything that might possibly cause her harm. She's my "baby girl," and I'm her "provider and protector."

This feeling, however, shows the great danger of living life by short, snappy little platitudes. In this complex and rapidly changing world, the pithy answers may work most of the time, or even for a season of time. But rarely, if ever, do those clever sayings, created by people, hold up across the board. (The words of Scripture, on the other hand, can be quite pithy, and they are trustworthy over time. But even these must be read within their proper meaning and context, or misunderstanding and even harm can result.) Seeing my daughter as "my baby girl" as she moves through adolescence, and seeing myself as her ultimate

## From Dee
### Memories of an Adult Daughter

This chapter was hard for me because my dad was neither a friend nor a protector. I know it's important for a daughter to forgive and get past her father's weaknesses, recognizing that no one can be everything we need, but my dad filled neither role for me. And even had my dad been a protector, one who was more interested in socially strangling me than in walking beside me, that wouldn't have been helpful. For a variety of reasons, I was ready to spread my wings fairly young in my adolescence. But I'm convinced that as a girl, and then as an emerging woman, many times I definitely needed a friend.

I think this is true for most girls. The older we get, the less we want and need a father to bail us out or make sure we're shielded from the world. We daughters know that over time we must take our turn to learn how to take care of ourselves

*(continued)*

"provider and protector" are two such sayings that must be examined for the health and well-being of my daughter.

First of all, when your daughter hits adolescence, she is no longer a baby. To call her that, even in jest or as a favorite pet name, may actually place a ceiling on her growth as a young woman. I can hear groans of disagreement: "But it's just a nickname" or "She likes it when I call her that!" As endearing as one of these names may sound, there is a negative suggestive power in such words. Each time the word *baby* is applied to your daughter, the message is reinforced that she's precious to you only if she remains your little baby. Other terms and nicknames have similar consequences. The older your daughter gets, it's best to work hard at avoiding these self-limiting terms.

I recall a scene from an otherwise obscure movie from the 1960s in which a woman in her fifties was constantly referred to as "Baby" by her elderly yet feisty shut-in father. The obvious point of this subplot centered around the relational stranglehold her father used on her even after so many years. Sure, calling your thirteen-year-old "Baby" or "Sweetheart" may seem innocent. The truth is that every time you use those words — or words like them — to express your relationship to her, you are holding her back from becoming a mature adult peer. At thirteen, this may not seem important. But remember that your main job as a dad is to set your daughter free to become an adult and an interdependent member of the family system by the time she is eighteen or nineteen years old. Every advantage you can give her—even small ones like what name you call her—will be a valuable gift to advance her journey toward adulthood.

Ask yourself this question: "If my daughter were a CEO of a Fortune 500 company, would I call her the name that I now use for her?" She may like the name and even feel that it brings a certain sense of reassurance and comfort. But as she grows, your role in her life needs to change. It's important for you to become more of a valued friend who takes her seriously, and less of a father who protects her and holds the world together for her.

The second popular wisdom that can hinder a daughter's growth into healthy adulthood is the notion of her father being her ultimate "provider and protector." We are all too aware of the strong and positive emotions such a role brings to many fathers. After all, isn't that the father's job in the family? Doesn't the Bible tell fathers that they have the ultimate responsibility to lead, provide for, and protect their families?

Actually, the Bible is silent on the specific *nature* of the father's role. Most commentators acknowledge that, while this is an important relationship within the

(within reason, of course). The role of protector may be a father's first instinct, but being a friend is a father's first (and last) calling when it comes to raising his teenage daughter.

If your daughter doesn't feel like you are her friend, she will likely feel forced to look for a man to meet that need. I know this is true; I am living proof. I gave my heart and my life to an older guy when I was sixteen because *I was looking for a man to comfort me, care for me, and cherish me as a dear, intimate friend!* I was never fully satisfied in that relationship, and I often felt guilty, but I knew I needed a man.

Dad, your daughter needs you to be her friend. She needs a man who will encourage and comfort her as she goes through these years and beyond. The best protection you can give her is the love and tender care of a friend. This will be the shield she will take with her as she enters the world as an adult.

———

family, people in biblical times had a well-defined understanding of the various family roles. Fathers in the New Testament era knew what was expected of them and what role they played with their kids. Strong evidence suggests that in biblical times, dads were significantly involved with their children and cared deeply about their kids as people. For example, in Mark 5, the synagogue ruler Jairus was distraught over the impending death of his twelve-year-old daughter. His plea to Jesus for help was far more passionate and nurturing than that of simply a distant "provider / protector." It was the cry of a parent whose love and compassion brought agony and grief to know that his daughter was suffering.

Your daughter needs you to care, to be involved, and to connect with her like a friend as she goes through adolescence. The difficult but necessary balance of being a father as your daughter grows up is that she needs you to give her encouragement and room to grow as a woman, yet she also needs to know that emotionally and relationally she really matters to you. If the latter is not evident, you may see her trying to hold on to the "feel" of being your "little princess."

> *Dear Dad,*
> *I love you so much but I feel like over the years we've lost a special connection between us. It seems like we never see each other anymore. Either I'm busy or you're busy. I just wish I could spend more time with you. I don't think it is fair to either of us.*
>
> —"Pumpkin," 13, San Diego, CA

Here are four ways that you can reinforce your willingness and desire to help launch your daughter into adulthood:

1. *Have a monthly "check-in" time to allow her to evaluate your relationship.* This may be frightening at first, but as you develop rapport and can sincerely and honestly talk and lis-

ten to your daughter, these check-ins can be incredibly powerful times.

We believe that fathers should "date" their daughters on a regular basis. But this check-in "date" is more like a business meeting between beloved colleagues. Instead of talking about life, sharing experiences, and connecting as people and friends, sit down, perhaps at a restaurant or in a park, and talk about trust, openness, and how you both are feeling about your relationship with each other.

This is the time for your daughter to share how she feels about her friendship with you. She may be feeling smothered. Or she may say that she doesn't think you trust her. She needs to have such a forum to talk to you, and you need to listen without becoming defensive. Let her talk. Bite your tongue when you want to interrupt, and let her know with every fiber of your being that what she has to say matters to you.

This is also the time for you to share your hopes, dreams, and fears. Let her know—honestly but gently—how you feel she's doing. If you've convinced her that you truly care about her and her feelings and thoughts, she will want to listen to you. She probably won't be too excited about hearing even a mild critique of her, so go slowly. But remember that she expects your authenticity, and she honestly wants to know what you think and feel. She will probably argue, get defensive, and tell you all the ways in which any seemingly negative perception is false. Don't get discouraged. She's trying out life, testing various values and patterns of behavior, and she's scared that she may be failing. She needs you to believe in her and encourage her.

2. *Look for positive signs that she's moving toward independence, and tell her you've noticed.* Because your daughter wants so badly to be affirmed by you, make it a habit to find specific and practical areas to affirm. If she's starting a new school year, ask her to tell you about her classes and let her know you'll be praying for her. When she hints at something new that she's

learned, or if she shows special interest in a specific subject, write her a note, telling her how terrific it is that she's growing up. It's the little things she's looking for as she seeks your approval and love.

3. *Ask her how you can help her.* Your daughter will appreciate a sincere attempt to care for her. But be careful. It's easy for this to appear fabricated or even loaded with unfair or overly protective expectations. You know your daughter. Trust yourself to know what will cause her to get defensive and what she will openly receive. Ask her, for example, how you can relieve some of the pressure she may be under. You may feel that she needs to "handle her own affairs" in order to learn, but she also needs to know how to let other people walk with her through life. It's an American—not Christian—value that claims we must "stand on our own two feet" and "make our way in the world" completely independent of others.

A healthy adult is not *independent* but *interdependent,* able to give and receive help from others throughout life. You can help your daughter to achieve this state. And if you really want to see her light up, ask her to help you! You type a paper, she makes some calls. As you work together as a team, she learns that she can help you as much as you can help her!

4. *Pray with and for her as often as possible.* As much as you want to protect your daughter, it is the Lord who is Protector and Provider *throughout her life!* Many dads believe their role is to be their daughters' protector until she gets married, and then they relinquish that responsibility to a husband. This philosophy—neither culturally universal nor even biblically sound—has the potential to do much more harm than good as a girl grows up. Proverbs 31 would not have been written if the woman described there had been raised by a father who was more interested in protecting his daughter than preparing her for life.

Earl Palmer, of University Presbyterian Church in Seattle,

once made the statement, "We as parents are not called to prepare the road for the child, but the child for the road." This is the task of a father with his daughter: He is to slowly remove his protective hand as she grows up, while replacing it with the loving advice of a friend. This is the only way she will learn how to protect herself from the wiles of a dark and aggressive culture. Prayer is the great reminder that we must relinquish our daughters to the protective and guiding hand of the heavenly Father.

What does it look like to move from being a protector to being a friend? Take a look at the following chart:

| Need | Protector | Friend |
|---|---|---|
| Identity | "I will take care of you; where would you be without me?" | "I like who you are." |
| Autonomy | "When you fail, I'll get you out of trouble." | "I'll be there if you need me, but I have confidence in you." |
| Trust | "You can count on me." | "I know you can handle it." |
| Communication | "Listen to me, I know what's best for you." | "I am here to listen to you; I will be your sounding board." |
| Closeness | "Stay close to me, I'll be your protector." | "Walk beside me, I'll be your friend." |

In looking at the five key needs of an adolescent daughter, here's what it means to be a friend instead of a protector:

### Identity

Most dads struggle with "letting go" of their daughters. You've watched your daughter grow up right before your eyes. As she's gone from a tiny and beautiful infant to a bouncing Brownie, she has always needed protection from a cold world that sought to do her harm. As hard as it is to set her free to live her life and make her own choices, she *needs* to be set free, and she longs for her dad to help cut the cord.

Do you like who your daughter is and who she is becoming? Tell her! Write her a poem or a story. Send her a card. Buy her a flower or an ice cream cone. Let her know that to you she is smart and wonderful, talented and lovely. As you do, continue to proactively hand this budding young woman off to the God who has pledged to be her *true* Protector, her faithful Lover, and all-sufficient Savior.

### Autonomy

A father-friend doesn't rescue his daughter every time she gets into trouble or difficulty. He encourages her to have the confidence to initially try to make it out of the hard time on her own. A father-friend is more concerned with his daughter learning how to navigate treacherous and frightening seas than he is about grabbing the wheel just in the nick of time.

Many parents secretly enjoy the power of knowing that their children would be in trouble without them. Some adults even continue to receive an allowance well into their adult years, *even when they have families of their own!* This dependency is neither healthy nor smart for the child and the parents. A child who has been allowed to run to her parents whenever things get tough is held back from truly becoming an adult.

We're not suggesting that you force your child to live on her own or that you never provide financial or other assistance as she grows up. In fact, once children have realized what it means to be an adult and are living responsibly and with a healthy sense of autonomy, occasional help can be an invaluable way of reminding them that, although they're adults, your relationship with them remains *interdependent*. Your daughter will always be a member of your family, and family members tangibly express their love and care for one another during both times of crisis and celebration.

A father-friend does not cut all ties and abandon his daughter as she gets older. We are suggesting a *balance* between two extremes, avoiding both the temptation to overprotect and rescue and the tendency to "cut her off." Your role must change from the father who protected and watched out for his little girl to a friend who is committed and available to love her, listen to her, and help her see that she's a capable young woman.

Sometimes a father can forget how much his daughter needs him as a friend during this process. A dad might, in trying to encourage his daughter's growing sense of autonomy, treat her as if she were really on her own. Such a strategy will backfire. If your daughter feels that she must be autonomous in order to receive encouragement, affirmation, and friendship from you, she will likely try to perform as an adult in external ways while she's not yet ready on the inside. Remember your goal as a father, which is to set her free as one who walks through life with a sense of inner confidence.

*Dad,*

*I love you, Dad, and I just wanted to tell you some feelings I've had for quite some time now. I want you to know I'm very proud of all that you have done for me. I thank you for teaching me how to be responsible, to strive for better and better every day, and most important, to put God first in my life. But, Dad, there were so many times all I wanted was a simple hug or just words of encouragement. I see you play with our nieces and nephews, and the love and affection you show them, and I wonder, where did I go wrong? I always have tried to be everything you ever wanted and I find myself still trying and never feeling good enough. I know you love me because Mom tells me, but sometimes that isn't enough.*

—Cathy, 25, Alexandria, VA

Cathy has spent a lifetime trying to win her dad's approval and affection. Because her effort was not developed from a healthy sense of self and in the knowledge that she was freely loved as she was, she never really developed a sense of personal autonomy at all. Cathy's father still had emotional hooks in her that held her back from becoming a healthy adult woman. If Cathy's father had worked to prove his friendship apart from her behavior and performance, and constantly reminded her that she was fully capable to make good decisions, she would be a different woman today. The good news is that if you are or were like Cathy's father—even if your daughter is grown—you can still affirm her ability to function as an adult (though it will take the same hard work we've outlined in this book).

### Trust

A friend trusts, a protector demands trust. A father-friend trusts his daughter, a father-protector expects his daughter to trust him.

While trust is a two-way street, and this duality is important in any intimate relationship, the giving of trust is also the defining of a new status in a relationship. Trust granted is a symbol that the relationship has achieved a level of equity and mutuality. When a parent demands trust, or even seeks it, "trust me" sounds more like a command of parental control, power, and authority than a desire for an intimate relationship.

We have talked a great deal about trust. It all comes down to a few simple questions. Do you believe that your daughter, as she nears the latter stage of adolescence, can handle her own life? Or do you feel that she still needs you and maybe her mother standing in the wings, ready to jump in and take over should she fall? To build the kind of friendship that will last a lifetime, and to develop a young woman who is capable and confident, you must believe that your daughter has the ability to take care of herself. Naturally, you will face times—as with any friendship—when you will need to "jump in and help bail." But most of the time you must seek to encourage her as a friend and allow her to increasingly live her own life. Your friendship, prayers, and support will provide her with a tremendous reservoir as she grows into womanhood.

## Communication

Fathers love to be consulted. In the psyche of the modern Western male, there is an innate need to be taken seriously. This means being viewed by others — especially our families — as a kind of Wizard of Oz, the All-Wise Answer Man.

What father doesn't envision himself offering eternal wisdom and spiritual insight? Yet every father is human, fallible, flawed. Whether or not he is willing to admit it, he knows it, his wife knows it, and his adolescent kids know it!

At a deeper level, most men would rather be themselves than carry the burden of being the "perfect" dad — whoever that is. We would like the relief of simply being travelers on the rocky road of life, along with our wives, our kids, our friends and neighbors, and the rest of the world. As such, we fathers need others every bit as much as they need us.

As your daughter grows up, you are the ultimate loser if you and she have not learned how to talk and share as people. Being her friend means letting her into the places in your life where few are allowed to go.

It's important not to reveal too much too soon because she is still in the transition period between being a girl and being a woman — a developmental peer. But you have the beautiful opportunity to *begin the process* during these vulnerable years. You can help her to see inside you — maybe just a little at first, until she is old enough to deal with you as a peer. This will enable her to trust you as more than a protective, authoritarian controller and see you as a person she can trust.

Dad, she longs to know you and to hear from you. A day will come when you will wish you'd spent more time simply talking from the heart. As your daughter proceeds through adolescence, she's ready for you to do that now.

## Closeness

We have stated that closeness is hard to describe and harder to define. However, the goal in your daughter's journey toward adulthood is for her to feel close to you. No one truly feels close to a protector, however kind and warm that protector may be. Rather, we feel close to those who have proven their friendship.

The little things you do as your daughter is growing up—taking her seriously, investing time and energy into caring for her, listening and talking with her, helping her find herself, and giving her permission to spread her wings and make her own choices—will all add up to her feeling close to you. It's not something you can order or schedule or turn on and off like a switch. It's not even a technique to follow, a kind of "five easy steps to becoming closer to your daughter" program. Everything we've been talking about in this book is more concerned with a mindset than a technique, a commitment than a strategy, a driving force than a calculated methodology of parenting.

Do you love your daughter? Be her friend. In turn, she will stay close to you. And you both will be the winners.

# CHAPTER TWELVE

# Setting Her Free

Dear Dad,

I'm sitting here on the beach at camp thinking about how lucky (blessed, I guess) I am, and I keep thinking of you (and Mom). You've always been such a great dad! Even when you were mad or upset you always made sure that I knew how much you loved me. Your constant praise for me, the way you believed in me (even when we both knew I'd made a mistake), and the friendship we shared, I took for granted all those years. Now I'm off to college in a few weeks, and it's suddenly hitting me how well you prepared me for the "big, bad world!" Until tonight, I don't think I'd ever really thought about what a gift you've given me as I've grown up. I'll always be grateful to God for the way you've cared for me, listened to me, given me advice without making me feel stupid or silly, and for how you've treated me like a close and precious friend. You are my friend, Daddy. Thank you for that!

—Mimi, 18, Cleveland, OH

In the Lewis and Dodd study of adolescent attitudes toward their fathers, they listed the "Top Ten Things My Father Did Right":[1]

10. Loved my mother
9. Was always there for me
8. Frequently told me he loved me
7. Always told the truth
6. Apologized when wrong
5. Really listened
4. Boldly talked about the Lord
3. Always had a sense of humor
2. Showed me how to be a Christian
1. Always put God first

Nearly every father wants to be the kind of man his daughter will be proud of. This list is a good reminder of that sort of dad. Love for your wife, commitment to your daughter, and genuine verbal and authentically fleshed-out faith are but markers that point to a man who cares deeply for his daughter.

Even when these adolescents reported "always put God first" at the bottom of the list, the rest of the list portrayed a father who is more concerned about living his faith than preaching it. The list describes the father who loves his daughter enough to be her friend, her teacher, and her guide.

## A Father's Role in the Adolescent Journey

By now you're familiar with the two key tasks that drive every adolescent: The

---

### From Dee
### Memories of an Adult Daughter

God powerfully met me as a broken and lost twenty-year-old woman who needed a father's touch. As you have read, my own father, because of many issues in his own life that he has yet to address, did not "set me free." In fact, at times I have thought that I've been even more powerfully set free by the mercy and compassion of my heavenly Father because my biological father left me to drift on my own. God has a way of healing the broken-hearted and fixing the mistakes and neglect of others.

But that, Dad, is not God's plan for your daughter. His desire is to have you be His channel of love, forgiveness, and empowerment for your little girl, now grown up. To set your daughter free, you must communicate three things to her with your life, your heart, and your words:

- You are my beloved child, and I will always be grateful for you.

*(continued)*

search for personal identity ("Who am I?") and the development of autonomy. As each young person deals with these tasks, there's no escaping the process of moving from being a dependent child to an interdependent adult. The ones who emerge from this trying and difficult season with the greatest sense of satisfaction and health will be those who have been supported by a strong perception of attachment to their parents. In most cases it is the father who holds the key to how well an adolescent handles the transition.

This seems to be harder for girls than for boys. Boys need to attach, or feel close, to their dads every bit as much as girls. But how they experience the relationship with their fathers is far different from girls. Boys want to be close, but that means they want to *do things* with their fathers and spend time with them in mutual activities.

A girl also wants to feel emotionally and relationally *close* with her dad, and she may accept activities with him as meeting part of that need, for a while. But what she's really interested in is having their hearts and souls connect. Boys want and need this at some level too, but few in our culture are aware of it. Girls are so in touch with relational dynamics, hidden meanings, and psychological innuendoes that from a daughter's perspective a father will either do a great job as a dad or he will fail miserably (there seems to be little middle ground). His daughter, by the nature of what she wants and needs, and how she sees the world, will not let the process happen any other way. Eventually a girl who has grown up disappointed in the way she

> - You are a gift of God, and I cherish the honor of being your father.
> - You are now a woman, and my role will change. From this day forward I will be your friend, your ally, and your champion.
>
> As you celebrate your daughter's movement into womanhood, you are handing her back to her true Father, who will be her Guide, Teacher, and Friend. It has been your task to be His ambassador, but when you set her free she becomes your peer in Christ.
>
> You will always be "Daddy," but she now needs to be able to look you in the eye and say, "I am a woman, called by God, blessed by family, and set free by my dad."

perceived her father ignoring her growing up may come to the conclusion that "that's just the way dad is," and internally make peace with her disappointment. But the years of trying to connect, to please him, and then the behavioral reactions when snubbed are difficult to erase. It can take women years to undo what a father did simply through ignorance or neglect.

Either way, a father has great power over his daughter. For most daughters, he holds the key to such life issues as self-esteem, career choices and ambition, relational stability, behavior and expectations in dating and marriage, and the ability to see herself as a fully functioning adult. Although most women can compensate to eventually overcome the gaps left by an indifferent or non-existent father, some are scarred for life. A loving, involved, attentive father can save his daughter from a lifetime of painful and destructive experiences. A girl who grows up with the perception that her father loves her, believes in her, trusts her, and celebrates the unique person that she is has a much better chance at reaching her God-given potential than one who is left to fend for herself.

One girl sent us a paper she had written for a class that described such a father:

My Father's Footsteps

I'm not sure my father understands how much he has made an impression on me. I live my life following his footsteps and trying to make each imprint fit. He is my guide and my most loved mentor.

I watch carefully the paths my father takes. With love and understanding, he works hard to see his children grow up to be successful, full of life, confident, and kind. The most important thing to him is knowing that his children understand the value of having an open and kind heart.

"Strive for your goals the way you know how, the way you know is right," he constantly tells us. It's simple, but not easy. Through struggles and hard times, my dad is a model for stability and peacefulness. He makes my worries vanish even during difficult times. His arm around my shoulder calms me and I feel safe. It is then that I can go out and do my best. He trusts in God, in himself, and in his decisions, and he leads his family to do the same.

## *A Father's Driving Goal: Setting His Daughter Free*

The ultimate goal of a father is to set his daughter free to be an adult peer in the family system. Some do this too early by pushing their daughters into adult-like roles and responsibilities before they are ready. Your daughter may seem ready to be treated as an adult, but you must be careful not to allow her to be pushed too quickly—even if she's the one doing the pushing! In our culture, many parents see maturity before it is actually there. As child psychiatrist David Elkind writes:

> The [historical but no longer culturally true] perception of adolescent immaturity, though it may have done a disservice to adolescents in some respects, nevertheless reinforced the unilateral authority of parents and adults. This authority guaranteed that adults would play a responsible role in helping young people meet the psychological, sexual, occupational, and cultural demands of their transition to adulthood. For [today's] postmodern generation, however, the perception of adolescent sophistication has encouraged mutual authority between young people, parents, and other adults. As a result, postmodern adolescents have much less support from the older generation in meeting the demands of the transition to a secure adulthood. And this, despite the fact that the demands for today's adolescents are much more difficult to satisfy than were those of the [earlier] modern era.[2]

The goal of parenting during this transition is to watch for the markers that indicate growth in the individuation process, specifically watching for identity formation and a growing and healthy sense of autonomy. The greater the growth observed, the more you should treat your daughter as an adult peer. Always be on the lookout for granting too much freedom, which can easily cause her to eventually feel lost and abandoned. The balance is difficult, but through careful observation, open communication, and genuine intimacy, common sense and intuition will be a reliable guide.

### Portrait of a Healthy Adult Daughter

There are six marks of a young woman who has been rooted and established by a father who is involved, attached, and caring.

*1. She is confident.* A daughter who has been raised by a father who takes seriously her needs of identity formation and autonomy, and who builds a relationship of trust, communication, and closeness will walk tall as a grown woman. She will believe that she can be whoever God calls her to be and do whatever God asks of her. She will take responsibility for her choices, recognize and admit fault when she is wrong, and expect everyone in her life to treat her with respect. This will most likely be true because that is how her father lived and how he taught her to live.

*2. She is compassionate.* A daughter who has been raised with a healthy sense of self will not be an adult who is overly preoccupied with herself, but instead cares about those who are hurting, unfortunate, oppressed. She will see life as a mission and calling. Her goal will not be self-fulfillment. Rather, she sees her life in light of who God is. Therefore, His priorities will be her priorities.

*3. She trusts and is trustworthy.* A daughter who has experienced adolescence in a two-way trust relationship with her father will reap the benefits of such a relationship firsthand. As an adult, she will know the power of trust and will be more likely to give herself to others who are likewise trusting and trustworthy. This is an invaluable asset when it comes to her future relationships. Her marriage, her friendships, and her career will be greatly enhanced because she understands loyalty and trust.

4. *She is a communicator.* A daughter raised to share her mind and heart with her father—who has experienced intellectual and verbal intimacy with a dad she trusts and loves— will have the ability to both expect and elicit the same from the future men in her life.

At some level, every man wants to connect with someone he loves, but many have been allowed to hide who they are for so long that they have lost the ability or skills to effectively communicate. A daughter who has lived with a communicating father will know how to draw out a man she cares about. She will also have enough self-respect to demand that he not hide from her. The chances of broken relationships in her life, due to poor communication, are far less than for a daughter who was raised by a silent or distant father.

5. *She will be a great parent.* The daughter who is attached to her father during adolescence will know the joy of intimate, relational parenting. Because she has lived with someone who saw her as important, valuable, and worth time and effort, she will follow that model into her parenting. She will also have the commitment to her own children that enables her to work with her husband to be the kind of father their children need.

6. *She will always be a connected daughter.* The greatest benefit of a daughter raised with an eye on father attachment is that the bond developed during these crucial years will be strengthened over time. As she grows into a woman, her appreciation for her father will only increase. And as the years progress, she will be able to see how deeply he loved her, even when she didn't seem to respond to him. She will be his number-one fan for the rest of their

lives. As she becomes more confident in who she is, she will also reconnect with her mother, and she will see her parents' partnership and love as the most powerful influence in her life.

### The Greatest Gift: What Teens Treasure Most in a Father

In Lewis and Dodd's study, teens were asked, "What do you treasure most in a father?" Included in this list was time spent together: "He's my best friend" and "He went out of his way to make memories." The list, however, can best be summarized by two simple phrases, "our mutual respect" and the "ability to talk about everything."[3]

These two statements are what we have tried to communicate throughout the pages of this book. To become the person God has created her to be, your daughter must know that you're there for her. She needs to know that you are calling her true self out, freeing her to learn how to make choices and live with them as she moves through adolescence. She needs to have a relationship built on mutual trust, communication, and a sense of closeness. As you love her, listen to her, and gently guide her through these years, you will provide her the best possible shot at life.

The last step in launching a daughter into adulthood is acknowledging to her that you now see her as an adult woman. There is no specific age when this happens; it may slowly evolve over time. One day you may be talking on the phone to your daughter and realize that she's no longer dependent upon you. She has developed into a person who knows who she is and is comfortable with herself and committed to taking responsibility for her life. When this happens, you will know that your daughter has crossed the line from child to healthy adult, from "little princess" to grown woman.

It's time to celebrate!

# Notes

**Chapter One: My Princess Is Growing Up**
1. For supporting studies, see L. Yablonski, *Fathers and Sons* (New York: Gardner Press, 1990); D. M. Alameida and N. L. Galambos, "Examining Father Involvement and the Quality of Father-Adolescent Relations," *Journal of Research on Adolescents* 1(2) (1991): 155-172; M.E. Lamb, *The Father's Role* (Hillsboro, N.J.: Lawrence Erlbaum, 1987); and J. Demos, "The Changing Faces of American Fatherhood: A New Exploration in Family History," in S. Cath, A. Gurwitt, and J. Ross, eds., *Father and Child: Developmental and Clinical Perspectives* (Boston: Little, Brown, 1982), pp.431-443.
2. Dr. Bruce Narramore, *Help! I'm a Parent* (Grand Rapids: Zondervan, 1995), p.15.

**Chapter Two: "I Need You, Daddy!"**
1. Terry Apter, *Altered Loves* (New York: St. Martin's Press, 1990), pp.74-75.

**Chapter Three: Trust: The Glue That Holds Relationships Together**
1. Doug Webster, *Dear Dad: If I Could Tell You Anything* (Nashville: Thomas Nelson, 1995), p.187.

**Chapter Four: Closeness: The Adolescent Safety Net**
1. W. A. Collins and S. A. Kuczaj, *Developmental Psychology: Childhood and Adolescence* (New York: Macmillan, 1991), p.108.
2. J. S. Turner and D. B. Helms, *Contemporary Adulthood* 4th ed. (Fort Worth, TX: Holt, Rinehart & Winston, 1989), pp.176, 178.
3. John W. Santrock, *Adolescence* (Dallas, TX: William C. Brown Publishers, 1990), p.227.
4. Carol Gilligan, *In a Different Voice: Psychological Theory and Women's Development* (Cambridge, MA: Harvard University Press, 1982), pp.156-157.
5. L. M. Brown and C. Gilligan, *Meeting at the Crossroads: The Landmark Book About the Turning Points in Girls' & Women's Lives* (New York: Ballantine Books, 1992), p.49.

**Chapter Five: Communication: The Heart of Father-Daughter Intimacy**
1. The research consistently affirms that a father is important in the life of his daughter (Turner & Helms, 1989; Papini, D. R. Roggman, L. A., 1992). Adolescent perceived attachment to parents in relation to competence, depression, and anxiety: A longitudinal study. *Journal of Early Adolescence,* 12(4), pp.420-440; Papini, D. R. Roggman, L. A. and Anderson, J. (1991). Early adolescent perceptions of attachment to mother and father: A test of emotional distancing and buffering hypotheses. *Journal of Early Adolescence,* 11(2), pp.258-275. Yet there is little focused research that attempts to understand how and why a girl's father is an important figure in her life as an individual. This is a question that has yet to be asked by family researchers on a systematic and consistent basis. One area, however, that surfaces in many of the studies on the parent-daughter relationship is a father's inability to communicate with his daughter in a manner as satisfying as communication

with her mother. Studies have found that there are some general communication problems between fathers and adolescent daughters (S. A. Anderson, 1990. Changes in parental adjustment and communication during the leaving home transition. *Journal of Social and Personal Relationships* (vol. 7), pp.47-68; D. M. Alameida & N. L. Galambos, 1991. Examining father involvement and the quality of father-adolescent relations. *Journal of Research on Adolescence* (vol. 1, number 2), pp.155-172.) Fathers are reported to possess less communication skill than mothers and to have, overall, more difficulty when engaging in interaction. But these data, again, are couched within father-child or parent-child studies and so often lump together boys' and girls' attitudes and perceptions. Nonetheless, studies do reflect this communicative attention in the father-daughter relationship. In studying parental attachment, for example, J. E. Paterson, J. Field, and J. Pryor (1994) (Adolescents perceptions of their attachment relationships with their mothers, fathers, and friends. *Journal of Youth and Adolescence* (vol. 23, number 5), pp.579-600) found that both sons and daughters "interact less with their fathers and report a lower quality of affect with them than with their mothers" (p.595). In a study on parental styles of parental communication, Reese and Fivush (1993) (Parental styles of talking about the past. *Developmental Psychology* (vol. 29, number 3), pp.596-606.) found that fathers put more "communicative pressure" (p.597) on their children than do mothers, although the authors believed this to be a positive parental strategy, helping the child to "prepare for communication with the outside world" (p.597). These and other studies found, in general, that fathers are less communicative with their daughters than are mothers (Bellinger & J. B. Gleason, 1982. Sex differences in parental directives to young children. *Sex Roles* (vol. 8), pp.1123-1139. R. W. Larson, 1993. Finding time for fatherhood: The emotional ecology of adolescent father interactions. *New Directions for Child Development*, (vol. 62) pp.7-25. B. McLaughlin, D. White, T. McDevitt, and R. Rasking 1983. Mothers' and fathers' speech to their young children: Similar or different? *Journal of Child Language* (vol. 10), pp.245-252. M. Malone and R. Guy, 1982. A comparison of mothers' and fathers' speech to their three year old sons. *Journal of Psycholinguistic Research* (vol. 11), pp.599-608.) As with much of the literature in this field of study, others have found no significant difference between mothers and fathers in adolescent communication (V. F. Haigler, H. D. Day, and D. D. Marshall, 1995. Parental Attachment and gender role identity. *Sex Roles* (vol. 33, number 3,4), pp.203-220.)

2. Henri Nouwen, *The Return of the Prodigal Son* (New York: Doubleday, 1992), p.90.

**Chapter Six: "Who Am I?" A Daughter's Search for Identity**

1. I had received this way of describing the Christian life from Henri J. M. Nouwen, who details this in his book *In the Name of Jesus*.

2. Robert Benson, *Between the Dreaming and the Coming True* (San Francisco:HarperCollins, 1996).

3. Santrock, *Adolescence*, p.386; see also study by H. P. Grotevant and C. R. Cooper, 1986. Individuation in family relationships. *Human Development* (vol. 29), pp.82-100.

4. Santrock, p.386

5. Patricia H. Davis, *Counseling Adolescent Girls* (Minneapolis: Augsburg Fortress, 1996), pp.30-31.

6. As quoted by Patricia Davis, *Counseling Adolescent Teenagers*, citing the work of Fine, Mortimer, and Roberts, 1990, p.13.

**Chapter Seven: Letting Go: Helping Her Become Autonomous**

1. F. Prose, "Confident at 11, Confused at 16," in W. A. Collins and S. A. Kuczaj, *Developmental Psychology: Childhood and Adolescence* (New York: Macmillan, 1991), p.385.

2. P. H. Mussen, J. J. Conger, J. Kagan, A. C. Huston, *Child Development and Personality*, 7th ed. (New York: Harper & Row, 1991), p.599.
3. Patricia H. Davis, *Counseling Adolescent Girls* (Minneapolis: Augsburg Fortress, 1996), p.56.
4. David Lewis and Carley Dodd, *"How Do Fathers Help Turn Their Teenagers' Hearts Toward Christ?"* (Abilene Christian University, 1997), p.80. The study was conducted with teenagers who were generally active in the Church of Christ. Although the findings cannot be universalized to all young people, or even to other denominations, as the Church of Christ is a tightly knit, historically uniform group, Drs. Lewis and Dodd detail some very important self-report data from the teenagers.
5. Lewis and Dodd, p.51.

### Chapter Eight: A Father's Love as a Model of the Father's Love

1. Gordon R. Lewis and Bruce A. Demarest, *Integrative Theology* (Grand Rapids: Zondervan, 1987), pp.195-196.
2. Henri J. M. Nouwen, *The Return of the Prodigal Son* (New York: Doubleday, 1992), p.90.
3. David Lewis and Carley Dodd, "How Do Fathers Help Turn Their Teenagers' Hearts Toward Christ?" (Abilene Christian University, 1997), p.81.

### Chapter Nine: Being Her Teacher When You Want to Be Her Judge

1. Patricia H. Davis, *Counseling Adolescent Girls* (Minneapolis: Augsburg Fortress, 1996), p.56.
2. Studies have consistently affirmed that communication problems exist between fathers and adolescent daughters. Fathers are reported to possess less communication skills than mothers and to have overall more difficulty when engaging in interaction with their adolescent children (see S. A. Anderson,

1990). Changes in parental adjustment and communication during the leaving home transition, *Journal of Social and Personal Relationships,* 7, 1990, pp.47-68; and D. M. Alameida and N. L. Galambos, "Examining Father Involvement and the Quality of Father-Adolescent Relations," *Journal of Research on Adolescence* 1(2) (1991): pp.155-172.

**Chapter Ten: Being Her Guide When You Want to Be Her Boss**
1. *Youthworker Journal* (March / April 1997): p.6.

**Chapter Twelve: Setting Her Free**
1. David Lewis and Carley Dodd, "How Do Fathers Help Turn Their Teenagers' Hearts Toward Christ?" (Abilene Christian University, 1997), p.76.
2. David Elkind, *Ties That Stress: The New Family Imbalance* (Harvard, Mass.: Harvard University Press, 1994), p.169.
3. Lewis and Dodd, p.75.

# Authors

CHAP CLARK is associate professor of youth and family ministries and director of youth ministry at Fuller Seminary. He earned his doctorate in human communication from Denver University where he specialized in organizational systems and family relationships. He is the author of numerous books, including *Next Time I Fall in Love, The Youthworker's Handbook to Family Ministry* (both Zondervan), *Boys to Men (Moody)*, and *The Performance Illusion* (NavPress), which was nominated for Christianity Today's 1993 Reader's Choice Book of the Year.

DEE CLARK is currently working on her master's degree in counseling at Denver Seminary. She has extensive experience in counseling and discipleship ministry with families, couples, women, and teens. She is a frequent conference speaker and has lectured at marriage, family, women's, and youth conferences across the country. With Chap, she is the author of *Let Me Ask You This* (NavPress), a marriage devotional.

The Clarks have been married for seventeen years and have three children. They live near Pasadena, California.

# PRACTICAL HELP FOR PARENTING YOUR TEENS

## Parenting Adolescents

There are some things about your teen that you can't change—no matter how much you'd like to. Learn to focus only on those things that are within your control to change.

***Parenting Adolescents***
(Kevin Huggins) $15

## Parenting Teens with Love and Logic

Need help with parenting now that your kids are in their teens? Learn how to parent with love and logic and be amazed at the great results!

***Parenting Teens with Love and Logic***
(Foster Cline & Jim Fay) $18

Get your copies today at your local bookstore, or call (800) 366-7788 and ask for offer **#2035**.